Road Bike Maintenance

Repairing and Maintaining the Modern Lightweight Bicycle

Rob Van der Plas

Illustrated by the author

Bicycle Books – San Francisco

Printed in Hong Kong

Published by:
Bicycle Books, Inc.
1282 - 7th Avenue
San Francisco, CA 94122

Distributed to the book trade by:
U.S.A.:   National Book Network, Lanham, MD
Canada: Raincoast Book Distribution, Vancouver, BC
U.K.:   Chris Lloyd Sales & Marketing Services, Poole, Dorset
Australia: Tower Books, Frenchs Forest, NSW

Photography:
Cover photograph by the author
Other photographs by the author and Neil van der Plas

Special thanks to:
A Bicycle Odyssey, Sausalito, California, and
American Cyclery, San Francisco, Califirnia
for their help and patience in lending us some
of the bicycles and components photographed.

Publisher's Cataloging in Publication Data

Van der Plas, Rob, 1938—
Road Bike Maintenance: repairing and maintaining the modern lightweight bicycle /
by Rob van der Plas.

128 p. 21.6 cm. Bibliography : p. Includes index.

ISBN 0-933201-79-6

1. Racing bicycles—Maintenance and repair.
2. Bicycles and bicycling—Handbooks, manuals, etc.
I. Title.
II. Authorship.

Library of Congress Catalog Card Number 96-84577

Table of Contents

Chapter 1

Know Your Road Bike

This book will help you keep your road bike in optimal condition. A road bike—that's one of those jobbies built for speed, with skinny tires and drop handlebars. If you ride a mountain bike, or any other type of bike, put this book right back on the shelf and look for one of our other books, such as *Mountain Bike Maintenance* or *Bicycle Repair Step by Step*, instead. And it's maintenance and repair that will be the focus of this book; you will find neither interesting detours into the secrets of racing, nor guidelines for riding techniques or equipment selection. But within the narrow scope defined by the title, this book gives you all the information you will need to keep your road bike running smoothly.

With the development of modern equipment, the difference between the components used on mountain bikes and road bikes has increased. Consequently, there is good justification for a book that specifically addresses the problems associated with road bikes only—and does that more thoroughly than would be possible in the context of a more general bicycle repair book.

Terminology

As with most of my works published by Bicycle Books, this book will be sold both in Britain and in the U.S.

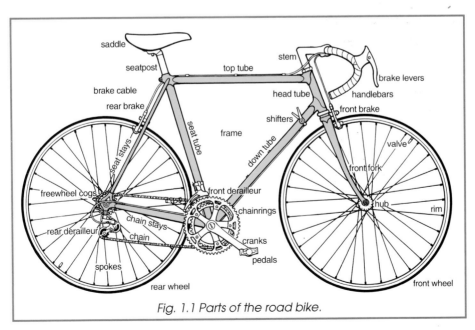

Fig. 1.1 Parts of the road bike.

And as always, there will be cases of different names for the same thing in the two cultures. I have made every effort to anticipate any such cases, though in general, I will be following U.S. spelling conventions. Thus, tire will stand for tyre, center for centre, and aluminum for aluminium.

Of course, the difference between British and American English often goes well beyond spelling alone: to give a few examples, braces become suspenders and spanners become wrenches as they travel from east to west across the Atlantic. Wherever relevant, I shall explain any different U.S. terms as well. And wherever the text remains unclear, I am offering a free copy of the next (revised) edition of the book to the person who first points it out to me (care of Bicycle Books—see the copyright page for address).

Left: road bike on work stand.
Right: front end with steering system.

The Parts of the Road Bike

To do any work on the bike, you need to know what the various components of the machine are called. Referring to Fig. 1.1, I shall now briefly describe the road bike and its major components. This is most easily done by examining the various functional groups of components one by one. Though not in the same sequence, that is the way the various repair operations will be grouped in individual chapters in the remaining parts of the book. The following functional groups may be distinguished:

☐ frame
☐ steering system
☐ saddle and seatpost
☐ wheels
☐ drivetrain
☐ gearing system
☐ brakes
☐ accessories

The Frame

The frame forms the backbone of the bicycle, on which the other components are installed by the manufacturer. It comprises the thick tubes of the main frame (head tube, top tube, downtube and seat tube), as well as the pairs of thinner tubes that make up the rear triangle: seat stays and chain stays. At the bottom, where the two parts meet, is the bottom bracket, and finally there are various smaller parts. Fortunately, the frame rarely needs repair work. And if it does get damaged, it's usually time to get a new bike.

The Steering System

The steering system comprises the parts that allow for balancing and steering the bike. These include the front fork, the handlebars, the stem, which connects the handlebars with the fork, and the headset bearings, which allow the steering system to pivot relative to the rest of the bike when the handlebars are turned.

The Saddle

The saddle is attached to the frame by means of the seatpost, which is clamped in the frame's seat tube by means of a binder bolt.

The Wheels

Road bike wheels have skinny high-pressure tires, enclosing an innertube. Two types of tires are in use: sew-ups and wired-ons. Usually, the tires are mounted on an aluminum rim that is held to the hub by means of a network of spokes, each hooked into a flange of the hub and screwed into a nipple at the rim. An alternative used on some high-end bikes, mainly those used for time-trialing, is the disk wheel, which will also be discussed. Whether spoked or disk, the wheel is held in the frame or the front fork at the hub by means of a quick-release mechanism.

The Drivetrain

The drivetrain comprises the parts that transmit the rider's propulsive

The road bike's drivetrain with crankset, pedals, chain, cassette freewheel, and front and rear derailleurs.

A typical gruppo, or group-set: an almost-complete set of components, this one is Campagnolo's Athena gruppo.

force to the rear wheel. It consists of the crankset, called chain-set in Britain, installed in the frame's bottom bracket shell, the pedals, the chain, the chainrings and the freewheel mechanism with cogs installed on the rear wheel hub.

The Gearing System

The gearing system comprises the front and rear derailleurs, which move the chain from one combination of chainring and cog to another, and the shift levers mounted either on the downtube or combined with the brake lever on the handlebars, as well as flexible cables that connect each shifter with its derailleur.

The Brakes

The brakes are operated from hand levers on the handlebars, to which they are connected by means of flexible control cables. When you pull the brake lever, the brake itself stops the wheel by squeezing two brake pads, or blocks, against the sides of the wheel rim.

Accessories

It's not fashionable to install much in the way of ancillary equipment on the modern road bike, the object being to keep the machine as light as possible. Just the same, the few items that can come in handy at some point will be discussed in Chapter 14.

Now that we have covered at least enough of the basic bicycle nomenclature to know what we are talking about, the next three chapters will be devoted to basics of bicycle care, before returning to the individual component groups of the bike in Chapters 5 through 14.

Chapter 2

Selecting Tools

In this chapter, I'll survey the most important tools required to work on the bike. Although it's possible to spend several thousand dollars on bicycle tools, I have found that at least 90% of all maintenance and repair work can be done with a very modest outfit. And even of those tools, only a few are so essential that they should also be taken along on most bike rides. The tools covered in this chapter include both regular, or universal, tools that can be bought at any hardware store, and specific bicycle tools that are available only from well-stocked bike shops (or specialized mail-order outlets).

Selecting Tools

Quality counts when buying tools even more than when dealing with most other products. I have found quite similar-looking tools at prices that varied by a factor of three—and in my youthful naiveté, I have only too often chosen the cheaper version. That's a mistake, because the tool that costs one third as much doesn't last even a third as long. Besides, it never fits as accurately, often leading to damage—both of the part handled and of the tool itself. After some unsatisfactory use, you'll probably decide to get the better tool anyway, so you finish up spending quite a bit more than you would have done buying the highest quality tool in the first place.

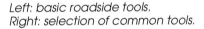

Left: basic roadside tools.
Right: selection of common tools.

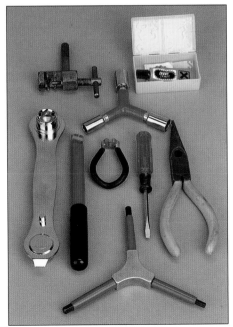

Having sworn to buy only the best tools for the job, we can now get down to a brief description of the various essential tools of both categories—universal tools and special bicycle tools. Even more uncommon items that are used only rarely, if at all, by the amateur bike mechanic, will be described in the chapters where their application becomes relevant.

Below, you will find most of the common tools described. Don't be discouraged by the length of the list, since you don't really need every one of the items described here. Refer to

the section on *Tools to Take Along* for the really essential tools that should be bought right away.

All the other tools can wait until you have a specific need. Road bike components are built with metric threading, and thus metric tool sizes will be required. The size quoted in mm (millimeters) will be the dimension across flats of the point where the tool fits—not the size of the screw thread, as is customary for American and Whitworth sizes.

Universal Tools

These are the basic tools that can be purchased in any hardware shop. I will point out which sizes are appropriate for road bike maintenance jobs.

Several different solutions with multipurpose tools, intended mainly for roadside work, including Park Y-wrench, Cannondale multi-Allen wrench, and Cool Tool. The latter with adaptors for headset and bottom bracket work.

Screwdrivers

The screwdriver's size is designated by the blade width at the end. You will need a small one with a 4 mm (3⁄16 in.) blade, a larger one with a 6–7 mm (1⁄4 in.–5⁄32 in.) blade, and one or two Phillips-head types for the screws with cross-shaped recesses instead of the conventional saw cut.

Crescent Wrench

Called an adjustable spanner in Britain, this tool is designated by its overall length. Get a 150 mm (6 in.) model and one that is at least 200 mm (8 in.), preferably even 250 mm (10 in.) long.

Box Wrenches

Known as ring spanners in the U.K., these are the most accurate tools for tightening or loosening nuts and bolts with hexagonal heads. Like all other fixed wrenches, they are designated by the across-flats dimension of the nut or bolt on which they fit. You will need sizes from 6 mm to 17 mm.

Open-Ended Wrenches

These are the most common wrenches available. They can be used when there is not enough access room for the box wrench. Get a set in sizes from 6 mm to 17 mm.

Combination Wrench

This type has a box wrench on one end and an open-ended wrench of the same size on the other. Even better than getting a set of each of the preceding items is to get two sets of combination wrenches, again in sizes from 6 mm to 17 mm.

Allen Wrenches

Referred to as Allen keys in Britain, these hexagonal L-shaped bars are used on the screws with hexagonal recesses often found on the modern bike. They are designated by the across-flats dimension. Initially you will at least need 4, 5, and 6 mm, but eventually you may also run into the sizes 2, 2.5, 3, 4.5, 7, 8, 9, and 10 mm.

Pliers

Occasionally you may find a use for a needle-nose pliers, diagonal cutters, and something like a vise-grip. However, don't be tempted to use any one of them whenever another, better fitting tool will do the job, since pliers often do more damage than necessary.

Hammers

These are classified by their weight. I suggest a 300 gram (10 oz.) metal-working model, which has a square head at one end and a wedge-shaped one at the other. In addition, you may need a mallet with a plastic head of about the same weight.

Hacksaw

When all else fails, you may find a need for one of these, e.g., to remove a tangled or rusted part or to provide a hold for the screwdriver in a damaged bolt. They are designated by their blade length. I find the 8-inch Eclipse saw quite adequate.

Files

These are designated by the length of their blade and their coarseness. For bicycle use, get a relatively fine 8-in. file to remove the occasional protruding spoke-end or a burr at the end of a part that is cut off or damaged.

Provisional Tools

These are last resort tools, should be avoided whenever possible, and should be used very carefully. They include some simple metal-working tools, like punch, drift, and cold chisel, that may be needed together with a hammer to tighten or loosen certain parts of the bike when no fitting tool is at hand. The cold chisel should be ground blunt, since you will not use it for its original purpose of cutting metal, but rather to unscrew a part with notches.

Special Bicycle Tools

The list of special bike tools that follows only includes the most common ones you are likely to need at some point. The list can be expanded almost ad infinitum, because so many special tools are available. Yet most work can be done with those discussed here.

When buying bike tools, especially the more specialized tooks, you will have to consult a bike mechanic to make sure you get the size or model of any particular tool that matches the parts installed on your bike. For that reason, it is best to have the bike with you whenever buying tools.

Pump

Although often considered an accessory, it is also an essential tool. Make sure you get a model that matches the particular valves used on your bike—all modern road bikes use the Presta valves shown below, as opposed to the Schrader type used on older machines, as described in Chapter 6). A CO_2 inflator will speed up the process, but each full tire inflation may require a new cartridge, so it's not much use except to speed things up when you are racing.

Pressure Gauge

In addition to the pump, I suggest you invest in a pressure gauge to make sure you inflate the tires correctly, at least to use at home—again matching the valve used on your bicycle's tires.

Tire Levers

Still referred to as tire irons in some circles in the U.S., these are now usually made of plastic. They are used to lift the tire off the rim in case of a flat (puncture) or when replacing tube or tire. Most road bike tires fit so tightly on the rim that you always need tire levers—usually all three. Select thin, flat ones that don't bend.

Tire Repair Kit

This contains most of the other essentials for fixing a puncture: patches, rubber solution, sandpaper. This little box also comes in handy to carry some other small spare parts, such as extra nuts and bolts, pump grommet, light bulbs, and the like.

Spoke Wrench

Called a nipple spanner in Britain, it is used to tighten, remove or install a spoke, either to replace it or in order to straighten a bent wheel. Make sure you get one that has at least one cut-out in the size that matches the spoke nipples used on your bike.

Crank Extractor

This tool is needed to tighten or loosen the cranks. Make sure you get a model that matches the cranks installed on your bike, since they vary from make to make, sometimes even from model to model.

Left: special tools for work on the headset.
Right: for really sophisticated work—torque wrenches to assure controlled tightening.

Freewheel or Cassette Tool

Used to remove a freewheel block (on older bikes) or to disassemble the cassette (on newer bikes) from the rear hub, which may be necessary to replace something as basic as a broken spoke. This tool must also be selected to match the particular freewheel used.

Chain Whip

On older bikes with a screwed-on freewheel, this device is used to remove individual sprockets from the freewheel. Depending on the kind of freewheel on the bike, you may either need two or one in conjunction with the manufacturer's special wrench.

Chain Rivet Tool

This tool is used to remove a pin that connects the links of the (endless) chain, so it can be separated for maintenance.

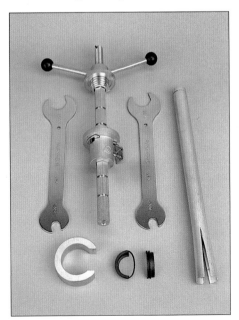

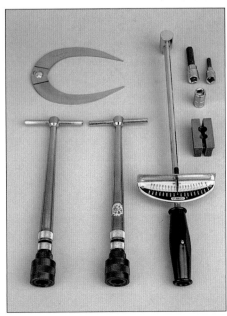

Cone Wrenches

These very flat open-ended wrenches are used to overhaul the bearings of a wheel hub. Available in several sizes—get two of each of the sizes needed for the hubs on your bike.

Bottom Bracket Tools

Needed for maintenance operations on the crankset or bottom bracket bearings. Many bikes are equipped with bottom brackets that need quite specific tools for this work; make sure to match the tools to the components on your bike.

Headset Tools

These are oversize, flat, open-ended wrenches, used to overhaul the steering system's headset bearings.

A selection of lubricants and cleaning aids.

Lubricants and Cleaning Aids

In addition to the tools listed above, you will need some materials to help you clean and lubricate the bike and its parts. Use the following items:

Cloths

You'll need at least one clean and one greasy rag. The latter is made by applying wax, vaseline, or bearing grease to a clean, dry rag.

Brushes

Get two sizes, about 20 mm (¾ in.) and 40 mm (1½ in.) wide.

Solvent

Used to remove oil and grime. Choose either turpentine, kerosene, or a special biodegradable solvent.

Bearing Grease

You can get either the special kind sold under the brand name of a bicycle component manufacturer or any lithium-based bearing grease—the same stuff at a lower price. If possible, get it in a tube, rather than a can, so it stays clean.

Oil

You can get a whole range of special bicycle lubricants, but in a pinch you can use SAE 40 motor oil or SAE 60 gear oil for most lubricating jobs.

Containers

You'll need a flat container to catch drippings or to clean parts in.

Penetrating Oil

Get a spraycan of thin, penetrating lubricant, such as WD-40. This particular product is actually formulated as a water dispersant, but works fine for getting tight things loose while inhibiting corrosion. Wipe it off if you use it on aluminum, since it tends to mar the shiny aluminum finish if left on too long.

Chain Lube

Get a spraycan or a dispenser bottle of special chain lubricant.

Wax

Used to protect bare metal parts; any car wax will serve the purpose.

Cleaning Aids

Many cleaning jobs are done simply with a cloth and water, while some items may have to be cleaned with a mixture of solvent with about 5–10% mineral oil.

Tools to Take Along

Only a few of the tools listed above are so essential that you should carry them along on your rides. The following is just my personal preference for what to take on a long trip into the country; you may decide to take less if you are in an area with plenty of bike shops. And of course, if you are riding in a group, you can share tools—and the burden of carrying them. In addition to this list, refer to the section on spare parts below for other items that should be carried.

After you have had some experience, you may decide to expand or modify this list to include the items *you* are most comfortable with. Carry them in a bag tied to the bike (such as a saddle bag—select one that does not dangle freely; it should be strapped to the seatpost and the saddle). Alternately, you can make a pouch as illustrated, carried either in a bike bag or tied directly to a frame tube or under the saddle. Here's what I suggest taking along:

- [ ] pump or CO_2 inflator
- [ ] 4 mm screwdriver
- [ ] 2 or 3 tire levers
- [ ] tire patch kit
- [ ] 6-in. adjustable wrench
- [ ] 7–14 mm open-ended or box wrenches
- [ ] 4, 5, 6 mm Allen keys
- [ ] needle-nose pliers
- [ ] spoke wrench
- [ ] chain rivet tool
- [ ] crank extractor

Additional Items

In addition—depending on the length and the type of the ride—you may want to carry some of the spares listed in the next section. Equally important are the following items: a bottle of water installed on the bike, a tube of waterless hand cleaner, a rag, and a first aid kit, including a pair of scissors and a pocket knife, and perhaps some lubricant in a spraycan or a well-sealed bottle. Finally, carry a lock, in case you have to leave the bike behind while getting help.

Spare Parts

Here is a list of the spare parts you may find useful to carry on a longer trip. Just how many you carry is up to you. Adequate preventive maintenance will forestall almost all repairs that require an extensive spare-parts inventory. Here is my list:

☐ brake cable (inner cable only, long enough for rear brake)
☐ derailleur cable (inner cable only, long enough for rear derailleur)
☐ spokes with matching nipples, making sure they are the right length for both wheels
☐ hooked emergency spokes as described in Chapter 5 for the RH side of the rear wheel
☐ bolts, washers, and nuts in 4, 5, and 6 mm sizes
☐ grommet (rubber seal washer) for pump
☐ if you will be riding in the dark, light bulbs and batteries for front and rear light
☐ innertube

Workshop and Bike Support

When you are out on the road, you can't be picky, but when doing maintenance or repair work at home, I recommend you provide a minimum of organized workshop space. It needn't be a separate room, nor must it be a permanently designated location. But it should be adequately equipped for working on the bike.

The amount of space needed is quite modest: 2.10 m x 1.80 m (7 ft. x 6 ft.) is enough for any maintenance work ever done on the bike. As a minimum, you should equip this area with the tools and the cleaning and lubrication aids listed in the preceding chapter. In addition, you will need a workbench—although the kitchen counter or an old table will do. Ideally, you should install a sizable metalworking vise on the workbench, although most of the jobs described in this book can be carried out without.

Next, you will want a support for the bike. The best ones are freestanding devices or those mounted against the wall. I suggest you buy a special contraption to support the bike off the ground, such as the ones made by Park and Blackburn. In an emergency, you can turn the bike upside-down, after turning sensitive parts on the handlebars out of the way or while resting the handlebars off the ground if necessary to protect items mounted there.

Chapter 3

Handling Common Parts

This chapter is devoted to techniques for handling some basic mechanisms found frequently on modern bicycles. This includes quck-release mechanisms, screw-threaded connections in general, cables and their adjustment, as well as ball bearings and their adjustment and lubrication.

Quick-Releases

Quick-release mechanisms are used on the wheels to ease removal, and the same principle is used in the tensioning toggle for the brakes. Instead of holding the spindle by means of one or two nuts that are screwed down, a toggle lever is used, and the other end is held with a thumbnut.

The thumbnut is not intended to be used for tightening the connection, but merely to adjust it in such a way that twisting the lever tightens the whole connection firmly. Open the lever by twisting it, close it by twisting it back. If the connection does not hold, first place the lever in the *open* position, then tighten the thumbnut perhaps half a turn and try again, until the lever not only holds the part firmly, but can also be opened enough to allow removal or adjustment of the part in question.

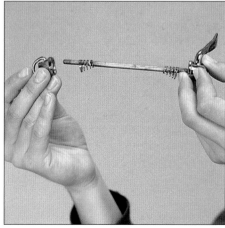

Quick-releases are used on the wheels and several other details. This is how to handle the quick-release: with both hands, one to adjust the thumbnut, the other to flip the lever.
Below: the skewer in detail.

Quick-release operation on the front wheel is often complicated on account of wheel-retention devices, installed to protect the ignorant from the pitfalls of incorrect quick-release use. If the wheel does not come out right away, check what is holding things up, unscrew the thumbnut further, and if necessary spread the fork apart or twist a clip out of the way.

Threaded Connections

Many of the bicycle's parts are attached, installed, and themselves constructed with threaded connections—not only nuts and bolts, but many other components as well. Essentially, all threaded connections are based on the same principle: a cylindrical (male) part is threaded into a corresponding hollow (female) part by means of matching helical grooves cut into each. When the one part is threaded fully into the other, the reaction force pushes the sides of male and female threads against one another, creating so much friction that the parts are no longer free to turn, thus keeping the connection firm.

Fig. 3.1 shows the details of a typical threaded connection, including an enlarged detail of a cross section through the thread. Screw threads are designated by their nominal size, measured in mm in the bicycle industry. In addition, the pitch, or number of threads per inch, and the thread angle may vary (either 55° or 60°). Finally, some parts have LH (left hand) threading, instead of the regular RH (right hand) thread. LH thread is found on the LH pedal, as well as on a few bearing parts.

Regular nuts and bolts are standardized—for a given nominal diameter, they will have the same pitch and the same thread angle, and they all have RH thread. Many other bicycle components are less standardized: there are at least three different industry standards for such parts as headsets, bottom brackets and freewheels. Although most modern bikes are built to the BCI (British Cycle Institute) standard dimensions for most of their parts, some bikes may be built to Italian or French standards. In addition, some component manufacturers seem to have abandoned the idea of interchangeability altogether.

To avoid mismatching when buying a replacement, always take the part to be replaced, as well as a matching component to which it is threaded, to the bike store, so you can try it out before you take it home.

Whether we are talking about a regular nut and bolt or any other threaded part, the way to loosen and tighten the connection is the same. One part has to be restrained, while

Fig. 3.1 Screw-thread details.

the other is turned relative to it—to the right to tighten, to the left to loosen in the case of regular RH thread; the other way round for LH thread. The lower detail of Fig. 3.1 shows how to tell them apart if they are not marked. Select tools that fit exactly to give the best possible hold and to minimize damage. Use a tool that offers some leverage (e.g., a wrench with a long handle) on the part that is turned, while the part that is merely restrained may be held with less leverage (e.g., a screwdriver).

All threaded connections should be clean and lightly greased when they are installed. If you have difficulty loosening a connection, first squirt some penetrating oil, such as WD-40, at any accessible point where the male part disappears into the female part, and wait 1 or 2 minutes before proceeding. A plain washer should be installed between the two. This allows you to tighten the joint

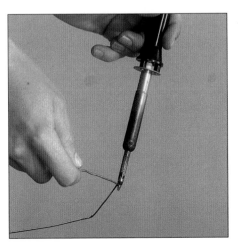

Cable details: Top left: the parts of the cable. Bottom left: soldering cut-off end. Top right: cutting the cable to length. Bottom right: crimping on an end-cap.

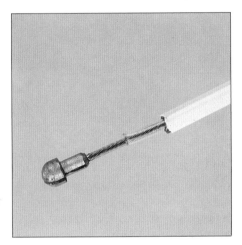

more firmly, while also making it easier to loosen.

To minimize the chances of a connection coming loose, usually as a result of vibrations while riding, many threaded connections are secured one way or another. Several different methods are used to achieve this: locknut, spring washer ,and locking insert nut. The locknut is a second nut that is tightened against the main nut, creating high friction forces in the threads working opposite ways. The spring washer expands to hold the connection when vibration would otherwise loosen it, and the locking insert nut has a nylon insert that is deformed by the threading, offering the required high resistance against loosening. If you have problems with parts coming loose, you may use any of these techniques to secure them.

A connection that comes loose frequently despite the use of such a locking device is probably worn to the point where replacement— usually of both parts—is in order.

Cable adjusting detail, here on a brake unit. The adjusting barrel is adjusted and held with the knurled nut.

Control Cables

Brakes and gears are operated via flexible cables that connect the brake and shift levers with the corresponding mechanism. The illustrations show details of a typical cable, including the pertinent adjusting mechanism. The inner cable takes up tension (pulling) forces, which are countered by the compression (pushing) forces taken up by the casing, or outer cable. To minimize the resistance of the inner cable running in the casing, the latter's length is minimized by having part of the inner cable run free between stops that are mounted on the bike's frame.

A nipple is soldered on at one end of the inner cable, while the other end is clamped in at the brake or gear mechanism. Ferrules are installed at the ends of the cable casing to provide a firm termination at the anchor points. There are several different cables on your bike, and you should take care to get the right kind. In addition to the different nipple shapes in use by different makers to match particular components, the thickness can vary. Usually an end cap is crimped (squeezed) around the free end of the inner cable—pull it off with pliers when replacing the cable.

The cables for index gearing controls are designed to be rather stiff so they can take up some compressive as well as tensile forces. The inner cables for brake controls must be quite thick to take up the high forces without stretching. Make sure the outer cable has the right diameter for the pertinent inner cable to slide through freely.

Conventional cables for the brakes and derailleurs should be cleaned and lubricated regularly, although most of them have a nylon liner, or sleeve, between inner and outer cable that reduces friction and keeps the cables running smoothly longer. If you live in a dusty climate, use only wax to lubricate, whereas grease is more appropriate in a damp environment.

To effectively lubricate a regular cable before it is installed, put some grease or wax on a rag and run this rag over the inner cable. Once the cable is installed, you may use a thickish spraycan lubricant, aiming with the nozzle at the points where the inner cable disappears into the outer casing. Remove excess lubricant with a rag to keep things as clean as possible.

Adjusting the cable tension is often necessary to adjust brakes or gears. To this purpose, an adjusting mechanism is generally installed at one end of the cable. Before attempting adjustment, make sure the cable end is clamped in firmly. To adjust, loosen the lock nut (usually a round knurled design) while restraining the adjusting barrel. Next, unscrew the adjusting barrel far enough to obtain the desired cable tension, and finally, tighten the locknut while holding the adjusting barrel to restrain it.

If the length of the adjusting barrel does not allow enough adjusting range, the inner cable must be clamped in at a different point. To do this, first loosen the locknut all the way while restraining the adjusting barrel, then screw the adjusting barrel in all the way, and finally clamp the cable in a new location, while keeping it pulled taut with the aid of a pair of pliers.

Ball Bearings

Virtually all moving parts rely on ball bearings to minimize friction and wear. They all work on the same principle, and their condition has a great effect on the bike's performance. Understanding their operation, maintenance, and adjustment is as important for every home bike mechanic as it is for the occasional cyclist.

Two kinds of bearings are in use, as shown in Fig. 3.2: cup-and-cone, or adjustable, bearings, and cartridge bearings (often referred to as sealed bearings). Although the latter are generally more accurate when new and can be better sealed against dirt and water, they are not inherently

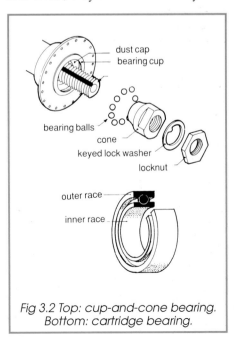

*Fig 3.2 Top: cup-and-cone bearing.
Bottom: cartridge bearing.*

Adjusting a wheel bearing using two wrenches simultaneously.

superior. Besides, there is little maintenance you can do on these models: either they run smoothly or they must be replaced, which is best left to a bike mechanic, since it generally requires special tools. Sometimes—but not usually— subsequent lubrication is allowed for by means of an oil hole or a grease nipple that is integrated into the part in which the bearings are installed. In other cases, the best you can do is to lift off the seal with a pointed object and apply grease.

The conventional cup-and-cone bearing consists of a cone-shaped and a cup-shaped bearing race, one of which is adjustable relative to the other by means of screw threading. The bearing balls lie in the recess between these two parts and are lubricated to minimize friction. Generally, bearing grease is used as a lubricant. Actually, oil—any thickish mineral oil—is even more effective, but can be messy, as it tends to leak out and has to be replenished frequently.

Regular grease lubrication should be repacked once a season. To do it, you have to disassemble the entire bearing, as explained in the relevant chapters. Clean and inspect all parts, replacing anything that appears to be damaged (corroded, pitted, or grooved). Then fill the cup-shaped bearing race with bearing grease and push the bearing balls in, leaving enough space to allow their free movement, followed by reassembly and subsequent adjustment. The bearing balls are often held in a retainer, and when overhauling a sticky bearing, it may help to replace them with loose balls.

Adjustable bearings must be so adjusted that the moving part is free to rotate with minimal friction, yet has no "play" (looseness). To adjust a cup-and-cone bearing, loosen the locknut or lockring while holding the underlying part (the cone in the case of a hub or a pedal, the cup in the case of a headset or bottom bracket). Next, lift the underlying lock washer, if installed, and tighten or loosen the threaded main bearing part (cone or cup) about ¼ turn at a time. Finally, hold that part again, while tightening the locknut or lockring.

Chapter 4

Preventive Maintenance

Most problems on your bike are avoidable if you regularly carry out a little preventive maintenance. It is actually very simple to keep the machine in good condition, so that it is working well whenever you ride it. That will eliminate the vast majority of repairs later on. Although most of the actual maintenance operations are covered in detail in the chapters that follow, this is the time to get familiar with a systematic schedule to check the bike. It is based on (almost) daily, monthly, and biannual checks.

Daily Inspection

This may seem to be overdoing it a little, but there are a few things you ought to look out for before you take the bike out for any ride. These are covered in this section.

Tires

Check whether the tires are inflated properly, considering the type of tire width and the road surface you will ride on: assuming 20–23 mm wide tires, you'll need 6–7 bar (90–100 psi) for smooth, hard asphalt; 4–5 bar (60–75 psi) for rough but hard surfaces; about 3 bar (45 psi) if you ride on dirt. Add about 1 bar (15 psi) to the relevant figures if your bike has very skinny tires that are less than 20 mm wide.

Handlebars

Make sure the handlebars are straight, at the right height, and clamped firmly—both in the head tube and in the stem.

Fig. 4.1
Lubrication points on the bicycle. Lubricate the points shown by a solid arrow with grease, those by a hollow arrow with spraycan oil.

25

Saddle

Verify that the saddle is straight, level, at the right height, and firmly in place.

Brakes

Check the effectiveness of the brakes by verifying that each can block the wheel against your weight while you try to push the bike forward with the lever depressed, leaving about 2 cm (¾ in.) between brake lever and handlebars.

Gears

Lift the rear wheel and, while turning the cranks, check whether the derailleurs can be shifted to reach all the gears—i.e., every combination of chainring and cog.

Monthly Inspection

At least once each month during the time you use the bike, clean it as explained below. Then carry out the same inspections listed above for the daily inspection, and in addition do the following.

Wheels

Check for broken spokes and wheel wobble: lift the wheel off the ground and turn it relatively slowly, keeping an eye on a fixed point such as the brake pads. If the wheel seems to wobble sideways relative to the fixed point, it should be trued (see Chapter 5).

Brakes

Observe what happens when you pull the brake levers forcefully: the brake pads must touch the side of the rim over their entire surface. Adjust the brake as outlined in Chapter 10 if they don't.

Tires

Check the tires for visible signs of wear, damage, and embedded objects. Remove anything that doesn't belong there and replace the tire if necessary.

Cranks

Using the wrench part of the crank extractor tool, pull the crank attachment bolts tight, as explained in Chapter 8.

General Inspection

Check all the other bolts and nuts to make sure they are tight, and verify whether all moving parts turn freely and all adjustments are correct. Repair or replace anything damaged or missing.

Lubrication

Lubricate the parts shown in Fig. 4.1, using the lubricants indicated below and wiping any excess off afterwards.

☐ For the chain, use special chain lube in a spraycan or a dispenser bottle.

☐ For the brake levers, pivots, and cable ends, use a light spraycan lubricant, aiming precisely with the little tubular nozzle installed on the spray head.

Annual Inspection

This is a complete overhauling job, which very nearly returns the bike to its as-bought condition. Treated this way, your bike will literally last a lifetime, unless of course you have a collision that destroys the frame. But even then, on a high-quality bike, it may be worthwhile to salvage most of the parts, replacing only what was actually damaged.

If you only use the bike in the fair-weather period, carry out this work at the end of the season. Then merely do a monthly inspection at the beginning of the next season.

First, carry out all the work described above for the monthly inspection, noting in particular which parts need special attention because they seem to be loose, worn, damaged, or missing. Then, work down the following list.

Wheels

With the wheels still installed, check for damage to the rim and the tire and for missing spokes, then remove the wheels.

Hubs

Check the hubs for play, wear, and tightness as explained in Chapter 5. Preferably disassemble and lubricate or overhaul the hubs, or inject grease if the hubs are equipped with some type of grease injector.

Chain

Remove the chain and measure the length of a 100-link section—replace the entire chain if it measures more than 51 in. (129.5 cm). The apparent stretch is a sign of wear that will affect shifting as well as the efficiency of the transmission. In addition, the worn chain will also

Left: checking the wheel attachment. Right: checking the brakes (or check while riding).

Cleaning in tight spots.

wear out the chainrings and the cogs. If the chain is not badly worn, just rinse it out in solvent, then lubricate it immediately (to prevent rust) and reinstall it.

Bottom Bracket

Check it for play and freedom of rotation. If the bottom bracket is of the adjustable type, remove the crank and disassemble and overhaul the bearings as explained in Chapter 8. If it has cartridge bearings that don't run smoothly any more, have the whole unit overhauled at a bike shop.

Headset

Try it out and make sure it rotates without play or rough spots. Preferably, disassemble and overhaul the bearings as described in Chapter 11.

Derailleurs

With the chain removed, clean, check, and lubricate both derailleur mechanisms, making sure the pivots work smoothly and the little wheels, or pulleys, of the rear derailleur turn freely. If necessary, overhaul or replace parts as shown in Chapter 9.

Cleaning the Bike

Do this job whenever your bike gets dirty—at least once a month in dry weather, more frequently if you also ride in bad weather.

Cleaning procedure:

1. If the bike is dry, wipe it with a soft brush or a rag to remove any dust and other dry dirt. If the bike—or the dirt that adheres to it—is wet, hose or sponge it down with plenty of clean water. Take care not to get water into any of the ball bearings, though.

2. Using a damp cloth, clean in all the hard-to-reach nooks and crannies. Wrap the cloth around a pointed object, like a screwdriver, to get into hidden places, such as between the cogs and the chainrings, underneath the brake arms, or at the derailleur pulleys.

3. Clean and dry with a clean, soft, dry cloth.

4. With a clean wax- or vaseline-soaked cloth, treat all the bare metal areas very sparingly.

5. Once or twice a year, apply either regular car wax or special bike wax to the paintwork.

CHAPTER 5

The Wheels

Wheel problems are the primary cause of bicycle breakdowns. In this chapter we shall cover all the major maintenance and repair operations required. The bicycle wheel consists of hub, rim, tire, tube, and spokes. One end of the spokes is hooked onto the hub flange, and the other end is connected with the rim by means of a screwed-on nipple. This chapter is devoted to the wheel itself, while tire-related work is treated separately in Chapter 6, followed in Chapter 7 by the subject of wheel building. First you will be shown how to replace the wheel most effectively, as is often necessary to transport the bike or to carry out other maintenance jobs.

Replacing Wheel with Quick-Release (QR)

Tools and equipment:

cloth (needed for rear wheel only)

Removal procedure:

1. If you are working on the rear wheel, first put the chain on the smallest cog in the back and the small chainring in front. That is done by means of the derailleur, while turning the cranks with the wheel raised off the ground.

2. If your tire is flat, it will easily pass through the brake pads.

3. To allow an inflated tire to pass between the brake pads, release the brake by flipping the brake quick-release.

4. Twist the hub's quick-release lever to the *open* position.

5. On the rear wheel, pull back the derailleur and the chain, using a rag to keep your hands clean. Pull out the wheel, guiding it past the brake pads.

Installation procedure:

1. If you are working on the rear wheel, first put the shifters in the position to engage the gear with the chain on the smallest cog and the small chainring. Turn the cranks forward if you have to engage another chainring in the front.

Installing wheel with quick-release.

2. To allow the tire to pass between the brake shoes, make sure the brake is released—if not, release the QR lever on the brake.

3. Twist the lever on the hub's quick-release to the open position.

4. On the rear wheel, pull back the derailleur and the chain.

5. Slide the wheel back into position, guiding it past the brake pads.

6. Straighten the wheel exactly between fork blades or chain stays and seat stays.

7. Holding the wheel in the correct position, flip the quick-release lever to the *closed* position and make sure the wheel is locked firmly in place.

8. Verify that you have installed the wheel perfectly centered.

9. Tension the brake with the QR mechanism, then readjust it.

Wheels Without Quick-Release

On tandem bikes, but also on some older regular road bikes (even quite good road bikes built up to 1970 and cheap ones up to 1985), the wheels are attached by means of axle nuts instead of a quick-release. Here's how to go about removing and installing such a wheel. You'll need at least one, preferably two wrenches to fit the axle nuts (usually 13 mm for the front wheel, 15 mm for the rear).

Follow the same preparatory steps 1 and 2. Then use the wrenches to undo, and later to install the nuts, making sure you install the washers on the outside of the frame or the

fork, directly under the nuts. If the wheel is crooked, loosen and retighten the nuts with the wheel in the correct position. Finally, check the brake as in step 9 above.

The Hub

Hubs should be checked occasionally to make sure they still turn freely and are not too loose. Maintenance will consist of adjustment, lubrication and overhauling when necessary. Cartridge hubs require specialized tools; some are adjustable.

You can maximize the life of a hub by means of regular checks, adjustment, lubrication, and overhauling. To replace a hub, the entire wheel has to be rebuilt, which runs the bill up considerably. Besides, many hub models are only available in pairs, effectively doubling the cost.

Checking Hub Bearings

This procedure applies to any kind of hub, whether it is the conventional adjustable bearing type or a cartridge-bearing model.

Tools and equipment:

Usually none required.

Procedure:

1. To check whether the hub runs freely, merely lift the wheel off the ground and let it spin slowly. It should rotate several times and then oscillate gradually into a motionless state with the (slightly heavier) valve at the bottom. If it

does not turn freely, the bearings should be adjusted to loosen them.

2. To check whether there is play in the bearings, grab the rim close to the brake with one hand, while holding at the fork or the stays with the other, and try to push it sideways in both directions. If it moves loosely, the bearing should be tightened somewhat.

Adjusting Hub Bearings

Carry out this work when the preceding test indicates a need for readjustment. In the case of a rear hub, you may have to remove the freewheel block first to gain access to the RH bearing. Tighten the locknut on the drive side (RH side) firmly up against the underlying cone.

Tools and equipment:

13–16 mm cone wrenches; 13–16 mm open-ended wrenches

Procedure:

1. Remove the wheel or, if it has axle nuts, loosen the axle nut on one side if you want to leave the wheel installed on the bike.

2. Loosen the locknut on one side by one turn, countering by holding the cone on the same side of the wheel with the cone wrench.

3. Tighten or loosen the cone by about a quarter turn at a time until the bearing is just a little loose. To loosen, counter at the cone on the other side with an open-ended wrench. To tighten,

counter at the locknut on the other side.

4. Hold the cone with the cone wrench and tighten the locknut hard up against it, which will slightly decrease the play.

5. Check and readjust if necessary.

6. Reinstall the wheel on the bike —or just tighten the axle nut if you loosened it on one side only.

Lubricating or Overhauling Hub

Once a season, or when adjusting does not solve the problems, lubricate the hub thoroughly as described here.

Tools and equipment:

13–16 mm cone wrenches; 13–15 mm box or open-ended wrenches; cloths; bearing grease

Adjusting wheel hub bearing.

Dismantling procedure:

1. Remove the wheel from the bike.

2. Remove the quick-release or the axle nuts and washers.

3. Remove the locknut on one side, countering by holding the cone on the *same* side.

4. Lift off the lock washer.

5. Remove the cone, countering by holding the cone on the *other* side. Catch the bearing balls as you remove the cone.

6. Pull the axle (with the other cone, washer and locknut still installed at the other end) out of the hub shell, again catching the bearing balls and removing the plastic seal (if installed) from the hub shell.

Overhauling procedure:

1. Clean and inspect all bearing parts.

2. Replace the bearing balls with new ones of the same size, and replace any other parts that may be damaged, as evidenced by pitted, grooved, or corroded surfaces.

Reassembly procedure:

1. First fill the clean bearing cups in the hub with bearing grease, then reinstall the dust seals.

2. Push the bearing balls into the grease, filling the circumference but leaving enough space for bearings to move freely. A rule of thumb is to use one ball less than might fill the cup.

3. Insert the axle with one cone, washer and locknut still installed. If you are working on a rear wheel, make sure it goes the same way round as it was originally.

4. Screw the other cone onto the free axle end, until the bearings seem just a little loose.

5. Install the lock washer with its key in the axle groove.

6. Screw the locknut on and tighten it against the cone.

7. Check and, if necessary, adjust the bearing as described above until it runs well.

8. Reinstall the wheel on the bike.

Notes:

1. If you replace the cones, make sure the axle protrudes equally far on both sides—reposition both cones and locknuts to achieve this if necessary.

2. Bearings that are packed with grease should not be lubricated with oil, because the oil flushes out the grease, rather than acting as a lubricant. However, some hub designs can be lubricated with a grease gun.

Rim and Spokes

These two parts have to be treated together, since the spoke tension determines largely whether the rim is straight and true or not. The spokes connect the rim to the hub in one of the patterns referred to as radial, 2-cross, 3-cross, and 4-cross spoking, respectively. Almost any pattern is suitable for the front wheel, which does not transmit any torque; the rear wheel should have a 3- or 4-cross pattern, at least on the RH, or chain side. If you are a heavy rider or ride on rough roads, don't use wheels with fewer than 36 spokes—at least in the rear.

For road bikes, two different types of rims are in use, depending on the type of tire installed. Tubular tires ("sew-ups") call for a so-called sprint rim, which has a very shallow rim bed, while the now almost universal wired-on ("clincher") tires, with separate inner tube, are installed on deep-bedded tires of the Endrick design.

The way to minimize wheel problems, most typically broken spokes and bent rims, is to keep the spokes tensioned adequately. Check the feel and the sound of plucking a well-tensioned new wheel at a bike shop and compare yours. If necessary, increase the tension of all or some spokes, following the procedure outlined in the following section on wheel truing.

Wheel Truing Check

When a wheel is damaged, the rim is often permanently deformed sideways, resulting in wheel wobble. This can be detected as lateral oscillations when riding. It may be verified by turning the wheel slowly while it is lifted off the ground, observing the distance between the rim and a fixed point on the frame's rear triangle, for a rear wheel, or on the fork, for a front wheel. On a properly trued wheel, this distance is the same on both sides of the wheel and does not vary as the wheel is turned.

Emergency Repair of Buckled Wheel

Sometimes the damage is so serious that you don't need to check: it will be obvious that the wheel is buckled — and there is little you can do to solve the problem permanently or even temporarily with certainty. Just the same, such a seriously bent wheel can often be straightened enough to ride home—carefully.

Support the rim at the low point and push down forcefully on the high points. Check frequently and continue until the whole thing at least looks like a wheel. Then follow the procedure for *Wheel Truing* to fine-tune the wheel far enough to be

Spoke adjustment.

able to ride it home. Have it corrected or replaced as soon as possible.

Wheel Truing and Stress Relieving

This is the work done to get a bent wheel back into shape. It is most easily done at home, but can be carried out after a fashion by the roadside—at least well enough to get you home. In the home workshop, it is preferable to do this job using a truing stand, but it can be done with the wheel in the frame, preferably with the bike upside-down (but with the handlebars supported so nothing gets damaged). It's best to remove the tire and the tube first, but this is not essential.

Tools and equipment:

spoke wrench

Procedure:

1. Slowly spin the wheel while watching a fixed reference point on both sides, such as the gauge on the truing stand—or the bicycle's brake pads if you are working without a truing stand. Mark the locations that have to be moved further to the left or to the right.

2. Using the spoke wrench, loosen the nipples of the spokes on the high side in the area of a high spot, and tighten those on the opposite side, in the same area. Turn the ones in the middle of the high spot ½ turn, and those further from the center only ¼ turn at a time (this is easy, since the nipples have a square flattened area for the tool).

3. Your wheel must be properly centered once you have trued it. This is checked by using a special "dishing" tool or the brake pads for a reference point. If the wheel is off center, tighten all the spokes on one side in ¼-turn steps, and loosen the opposing spokes in ¼-turn steps to center the rim on the axle. Always begin and end at the valve hole so you don't miss any spokes.

4. Once you have achieved an improved spoke line, you must relieve stress on the spokes. This is done by grasping parallel spoke pairs on both sides of the wheel and squeezing them together working around the wheel, starting and finishing at the valve hole.

5. Continue this process for each off-set area, checking and correcting frequently, until the wheel is quite well trued.

6. On the rear wheel of a derailleur bike, the spokes on the RH side will be under a steeper angle, and consequently under a higher tension, than those on the LH side. This is on account of the asymmetry of the hub flanges owing to the freewheel block on the RH side.

Note:

The first time you true a wheel, it will take forever and a day and still may not lead to a really satisfactory result. Persist, and the next time will be easier. Just the same, the first few times you do this, have a bike mechanic check your work.

Replacing Individual Spokes

Sometimes a spoke breaks—usually at the head, which is hooked in at the hub flange. Make sure you have replacement spokes of the same thickness and the same length.

Tools and equipment:

spoke wrench; tools to remove freewheel block or sprockets of cassette hub

Procedure:

1. Remove freewheel block or freewheel cassette (refer to Chapter 8), tire, tube, and rim tape. Unscrew nipple of broken spoke with nipple wrench.

2. Hook the spoke through the hole in the hub—with the head on the inside of the flange if this is an outside spoke, on the outside if it is an inside spoke.

3. Count four spokes along the circumference of the rim to find a spoke that is routed the same way as your spoke will be. Refer to this one to find out just how to run it and how it should cross which of the other spokes.

4. Route your spoke the same way as the example.

5. Screw the nipple onto the threaded end of the spoke, slowly increasing tension until it is about as tight as all other spokes on the same side of the same wheel.

6. Follow the procedure given under *Wheel Truing* until the wheel is perfectly true.

7. Replace tire, tube, and rim tape. Inflate the tire.

Left: stress-relieving a group of spokes. Right: 3-bladed semi-disk wheel.

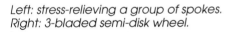

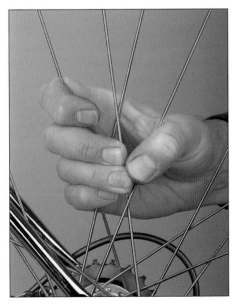

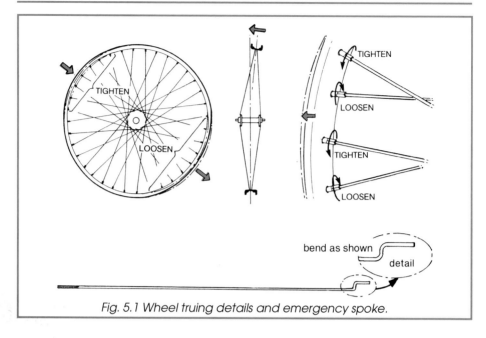

Fig. 5.1 Wheel truing details and emergency spoke.

Note:

If only one spoke is broken, and you don't have a spare spoke, true the wheel around the broken spoke by tightening and loosening the opposing sides. Stress-relieve the wheel, then true it again. If several spokes are broken, figure out which rim hole goes with which hub hole by observing that every fourth spoke along the rim (and every second one on the same hub flange) runs similarly.

Emergency Spoke Installation

Make an emergency spoke by bending an oversized spoke from which you remove the head to form a hook at one end. This is useful when a spoke on the RH side of the rear wheel breaks, since it can be hooked in without removing the freewheel.

Note:

When you get home, replace this temporary repair with a permanent spoke of the right length, a job you can either do yourself or leave to the bike shop. Warning: an improperly tensioned wheel can go out of true quickly or even collapse, especially if the spokes are too loose. Spokes tensioned too tightly will cause the rim to crack at the nipples.

Disk Wheels

Not much I can tell you about disk wheel maintenance. They're pretty strong and not likely to get damaged. And if they do, there's no way you can fix them. Don't use a chemical solvent (instead, use a citrus-based solvent) on disk wheels or any other composite part, because it softens the resin that bonds the fibers together.

CHAPTER 6

Tires and Tubes

The tires remain the bicycle's weak spot. I advise carrying a spare tube, a pump, and a repair kit at all times. Two different categories of tires are in use for bicycles: the wired-on tire (usually referred to as *clincher* in the U.S.), consisting of separate cover and innertube, and the tubular tire (referred to as *tub* in Britain, *sew-up* in the U.S.). The latter type is primarily used in racing; the former is the more universally used in training, and lately even in some racing events.

Tire Size

Tire and rim must be matched: narrow sprint rims are used to mount tubular tires, whereas wired-on clincher tires are mounted on Endrick, or deep-bedded, rims, often referred to as clincher rims. Many different diameters and widths of Endrick rims are available—along with matching tires.

Nowadays the French 700 C size is used pretty universally for road bikes, but older road bikes may have 27 x 1¼-in. tires. Whereas the 27-in. tire is mounted on a rim of 630 mm tire seat (or rim shoulder) diameter, the 700 C tire fits on a 62 mm rim. Rarely, you will find other sizes, such as 26 in. and 24 in. for the front wheel of special machines or on bikes intended for small riders.

This is about as far as I can go on the subject of tire sizing in what must primarily remain a repair manual. In the remaining sections of this chapter, I shall cover the various repair and replacement jobs associated with tires, tubes, and tubular tires.

Puncture Repair

More commonly referred to as "fixing a flat" in the U.S., this work is required more frequently than any other repair, and every cyclist should be able to handle this simple job. Whether you actually repair the old tube or install a new one is up to you, but you can't carry unlimited spares,

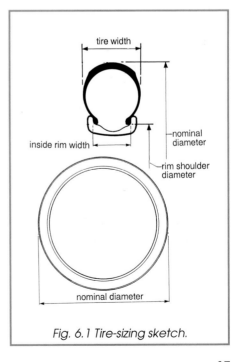

Fig. 6.1 Tire-sizing sketch.

so you will be confronted with the need to repair the leak yourself sooner or later. Though the description involves many steps, the work is not difficult and can, with some practice, be handled in about ten minutes, even out on the trail.

The whole thing is expedited considerably if the tire and rim match rather generously. That is typically taken care of by selecting rims with a deep bed and trying out the tire for fit.

Tools and equipment:

tire repair kit; tire levers; spare tube, if you want to replace tube

Procedure:

1. Check the valve. Try to inflate and check whether air is escaping there. Presta valves may leak if the top nut isn't screwed on. Sometimes a Schrader valve (quite common until the late 80s, but no longer used on modern road bikes) will leak and can be fixed by screwing in the interior, using a narrow object, like a small screwdriver.

2. Remove the wheel from the bike, holding back chain and rear derailleur, after having selected a gear that combines a small cog with a small chainring if you're dealing with a rear wheel. If necessary to clear the brakes, either compress the limp tire, or release the brake cable.

3. Check the circumference of the tire for visible signs of damage, and mark their location with a ballpoint pen or by tying

something around the nearest spoke.

4. If the tire still contains air, first unscrew the nut, then push the valve pin in. This will allow all trapped air to escape.

5. To loosen the tire, push one side of the tire towards the (deeper) center of the rim around the entire circumference of the wheel to loosen that side enough to ease removal.

6. If it does not come off by hand, place the longer end of a tire lever under the side of the tire and hook the short end under a spoke.

7. Two or three spokes further round the rim, insert the second tire lever.

8. If necessary, insert the third tire lever two or three spokes in the opposite direction (if it is necessary and you have only two levers, remove one of the two and use it in the new location).

9. Remove the tire levers and pull the rest of that side of the tire off by hand, working around, starting at the location of the tire levers.

10. Remove the tube from under the tire, pushing the valve out of the valve hole.

11. Check the tube, starting at any location you may have marked as an obvious or probable cause of the puncture.

12. If the leak is not easily detected, inflate the tire and check carefully for escaping air, passing the tube by your eye, which is your most

sensitive detection device. To date, I have not encountered a leak that could not be found this way, but it takes some practice.

13. If you are not able to detect escaping air, submerge the inflated tire in water or, if not enough of that is available, rub a little water from your water bottle over the inflated tire, systematically working around and reinflating the tire as required to maintain adequate pressure.

14. Mark the location of the leak.

15. Take an appropriate patch from the patch kit. Generally, the smallest size will do, except if you are dealing with several holes close together or with a long tear.

16. If necessary, dry the tube around the leak. Roughen the area around the leak with sandpaper from the patch kit and wipe clean.

17. Take a sizeable drop of rubber solution from the tube in the patch kit and quickly spread it smoothly and evenly over an area around the leak that is a little larger than the patch.

18. Allow the rubber solution to dry one minute for a normal butyl tube, twice that long if you have a latex tube.

19. Remove the plastic or aluminum foil from the adhesive side of the patch without touching the adhesive, and quickly yet accurately place the patch on the area prepared, centered at the leak.

20. Push the patch down, then knead and flex the patch and the tube together to make sure the patch

Inserting tire levers.

Removing tire by hand.

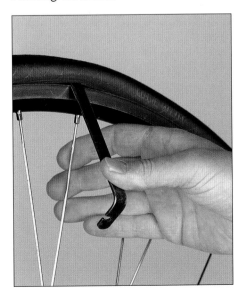

adheres fully. If not, remove it and restart at step 15.

21. Inflate the tube partially to establish whether air is still escaping. If it is, there may be another hole or the first one was not patched properly. Repeat the repair if necessary.

22. After you have inflated the tube, while waiting to verify whether it holds air, check the inside of the tire to find and remove any embedded objects that may have

caused the puncture—or may cause subsequent ones. Particularly tricky in some areas are thorns, which wear off to be invisible on the outside, yet protrude far enough inside to pierce the tube when the rubber of the tire is compressed.

23. Also check carefully inside the rim well to make sure none of the spokes protrude and that they are covered by rim tape. Once at home, file off any spokes that do

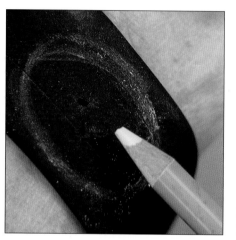

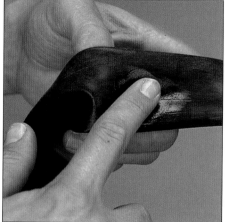

Top: marking the location of the hole.
Bottom: scraping the area.

Top: applying adhesive.
Bottom: applying the patch.

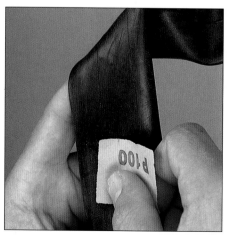

protrude, and replace or patch defective rim tape. Duct tape works nicely.

24. When you are sure the problem is solved, let most of the air escape from the tube until it is limp.

25. Starting at the valve, put the tube back under the tire, over the rim.

26. Starting opposite the valve and working in both directions towards it, carefully pull the side of the tire back over the rim.

27. If the tube has a Presta valve, reinstall the knurled locknut. Whatever the valve, make sure it is straight.

28. Partially inflate the tire and check once more to make sure the tube is not pinched, kneading the tire sidewalls from both sides, and make sure it is centered. The ridge on the side should be equally far from the rim around the circumference on both sides.

29. Inflate the tire to the desired pressure—the narrower the tire, the higher the pressure should be.

Note:

Even if you choose not to patch a tube while you are out on the road, replacing it with your spare tube instead, you should repair the puncture once you get home, so you can use that tube as a spare.

Replacing Tube or Tire

If the innertube cannot be repaired, because the hole is on a seam or too large, or if you want to install another tube for any other reason, proceed as described above for repairing a puncture under steps 2–10, then install the new tube and continue as described under steps 25–29.

To replace the tire casing itself, again proceed as described above in steps 2–10 for repairing a puncture. Then remove the other side of the tire in the same direction as the first side. Put one side of the new tire in place and continue as before.

Patching Tire Casing

Sometimes a tire casing that is damaged can be repaired at least temporarily. To do so, proceed just as you did for the puncture repair. Repair the inside of the tire, using a 2.5 x 5 cm (1 x 2 in.) "boot." This can be a piece of duct tape, a piece cut from the side of a discarded lightweight tire, or even a piece of plastic sheet if you're desperate. First put rubber solution on one side of the patch, allowing it to dry, and then reapply rubber solution there and in the area of the tire where it has to be repaired. Once it has adhered, generously sprinkle talcum powder over the area of the boot and around it to prevent the tire from sticking to the tube.

Tire Sealants and Other Tricks

Every few years some manufacturer claims to have solved the problem of the flat tire forever. The proposed solutions fall into three different categories: more-or-less solid tubes, tube sealants, and reinforced tire casings. All of them have some effect, but to date the perfect solution has not been offered.

The use of a sticky sealant, advertised under the name Green Slime in the U.S., has proven very effective against the problems associated with a straightforward puncture caused by glass or other sharp objects. Similar to the compound used to seal tubeless car tires, it builds up a sealing layer around and over the point where a leak starts to develop. I have never had a need for it (I get very few punctures because I ride carefully and avoid bad roads), but if you tend to get many punctures, you should probably invest in a bottle and squirt it into the tire while inflating it.

There is an inherent danger in the use of tire sealants: if the tire bursts, the sealant spills out and forms a perfect lubricant between your bike and the road—causing complete loss of control over the bike.

Solid innertubes have been offered before and have been found wanting, but the current crop is more interesting than its predecessors. Consisting of a plastic closed-cell foam material, these tubes are relatively light and flexible. Even the best of these things feels more dead than conventional pneumatic tires, and they are comfortable only where they are least needed—namely on perfectly smooth roads. On rough roads, they are very uncomfortable.

Finally, there are reinforced, or belted, tire casings. Typically these include a strip of very strong but reasonably flexible woven material between the regular casing fabric and the rubber tread. Even these only

prevent straight punctures, while they are of little or no help against the pervasive snakebite punctures, which are attributable to pinching the tube between the rim and the tire casing when riding over an obstacle. By and large, the most effective preventive measures remain careful riding and adequate inflation pressure.

Tubular Tires

These special racing tires are used less often today than they once were, mainly due to the inconvenience of repairing them. They are sewn around their tube and literally glued to a special rim.

Patching a tubular tire is a labor of love—if you have neither the patience to do it, nor the money to have someone else do it for you or to buy a new one each time you have a puncture, you'd be better off installing wired-on tires and matching rims.

Removing a tubular tire.

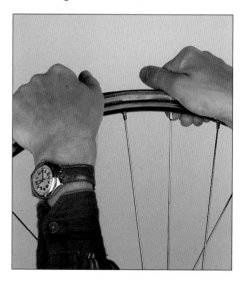

Removing Tubular Tires

To remove the tire when you have a puncture, first remove the wheel from the bike. Starting opposite the valve, roll off the tire with the palms of both hand, working around the tire in both directions; finally, remove the valve from the rim. When folding up the tire, take care to do it in such a way that the adhesive backing does not stick to itself.

Installing Tubular Tires

When you have a puncture, it is perfectly satisfactory to simply install the spare on the still-tacky rim, merely taking care not to corner so wildly that the thing might come off. For a permanent installation, proceed as follows:

Tools and equipment:

either: tube of tire adhesive, or: double-sided adhesive tire-mounting tape (the latter is easier to use; it is, however, hard to get in parts of the U.S., though readily available elsewhere); acetone or other solvent; pump

Procedure:

1. Clean off the old adhesive with acetone or remove the old adhesive tape.

2. When using adhesive compound: spread an even layer on the entire rim bed, subsequently cleaning your hands either with acetone or (preferably) with waterless hand cleaner.

3. When using adhesive tape: wrap the tape around the rim tightly, starting just before the valve hole and ending just after (i.e. overlapping at the valve hole), centering the tape carefully. Push it down with a firm rounded object like the handle of a screwdriver. Cut a hole for the valve, then remove the paper backing strip, also from the overlapped part.

4. Slightly moisten the adhesive rim bed, so the tire does not adhere, fully before it is properly positioned. Place a strip of paper, about two inches wide, opposite the valve hole; this will give you a good place to start removal of the tire when it has to be replaced later.

5. Inflate the tire somewhat. If you're installing a brand new tire, first stretch it, holding it down with your feet, as you pull the opposite end up forcefully with your hands.

6. Insert the valve, then place the tire on the rim, centering it properly as you work all around the rim (compare the concentricity of the sidewall).

7. Inflate to the final pressure, then check and correct concentricity once more. Remove any spilled adhesive and tear off the ends of the paper strip opposite the valve. Wait at least overnight before using the wheel, so the adhesive will be cured.

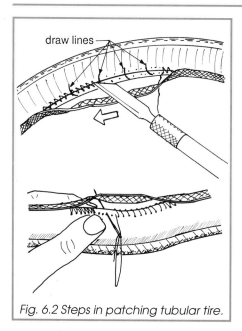

Fig. 6.2 Steps in patching tubular tire.

Repairing Tubular Tires

The instructions that follow are based on the assumption that the tire has been removed from the wheel—it's not a roadside repair but one to do at home.

Tools and equipment:

tubular tire patch kit (comprising patches, rubber solution, sandpaper, twine, needle, thimble, and talcum powder—often in the form of a stick which you scrape to obtain powder); sharp knife; pump

Proceaure:

1. Inflate the tire to find out where the hole is. Listen, or if you don't hear escaping air, pass the entire tire surface closely past your eyes, which are very sensitive; if this doesn't work either, submerge the tire in water, a section at a time, watching for escaping air bubbles. Mark the location of the leak.

2. Over an area about 4–5 inches either side of the leak, remove the backing tape, using a thin object.

3. Draw a ball-point line every half inch across the seam in the tire, then cut away the stitching over a length of about 6 inches, centered around the leak. Remove the loose remains of the stitching.

4. Dig the tube out from under the backing strip; repair the puncture as described for a regular puncture in *Puncture Repair*, steps 10–24 above.

5. Put the tube back in the cover, and pull the backing tape and the cover itself together, lining up the lines you had drawn before.

6. Holding back the tube so it will not get damaged, carefully sew together the seam, not pulling it so tight that it will not lie flat. Work the ends of the twine back under the stitching to prevent it from unraveling.

7. Using the regular rubber solution on the tire cover and the cover tape, glue the tape back into place.

Note:

Keep spare tubular tires in a cool, dry place, preferably inflated somewhat, and ideally installed around a spare rim. Don't forget to pack a spare when riding; release it from its tightly folded position for proper storage when you get home.

Chapter 7

Wheel Building

This is the post-graduate school of wheel maintenance, and you are not obliged to enroll—it's perfectly sensible to leave this kind of work to your friendly bike shop. However, for the ambitious home mechanic, there's nothing to beat wheel building for therapeutic value (if not for frustration, as it is to some).

Replacing Identical Rim

First, I will describe a simple method for replacing a rim with a new one using the old hub and spokes. For a more thorough treatment, required when the spokes or the hub must also be replaced, see the following section.

Make sure the new rim is identical to the old one: check the size and count the holes in the hub and the rim, and make sure the spoke holes are offset relative to the centerline of the rim in the same pattern (check both sides of the valve).

Tools and equipment:

spoke wrench; cloth; grease; adhesive tape

Procedure:

1. Remove the tire, the tube, and the rim tape from the old rim on the existing wheel.

2. Place the old tape on the new rim, with the valve holes lined up.

3. Tape the two rims together between the spoke holes in at least three locations.

4. Starting at the first spoke to the right of the valve hole, remove each spoke from the old rim, and immediately install it in the new rim. Screw the nipple on until about 3 mm (⅛ in.) of the spoke screw thread is exposed.

5. After all the spokes have been replaced, work your way around the wheel, tightening all the

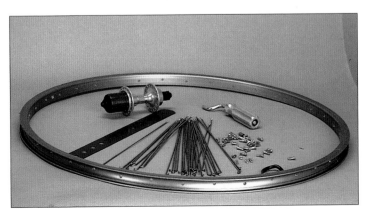

Spokes, hub, and rim. If only the rim is damaged, and the other parts are OK, you can follow the procedure, starting on this page. Otherwise, start all over, following Rebuilding a Wheel.

spokes in steps of about one turn until they are equally tensioned.

6. Follow the description for wheel truing to bring the wheel into lateral and radial true and to tension the spokes until they have about the same tension as those on a new wheel, paying attention to the need for higher tension on the freewheel side of a typical rear wheel.

7. Stress-relieve the spokes by grasping them in pairs of parallel spokes, working around the wheel. Center the wheel using a centering device if you have one, your brake pads if you do not. Tension and true the spokes again, if necessary.

8. Check inside the rim and file off any spoke ends that may project from the nipples.

9. Install the new rim tape, the tire and the tube. Inflate the tire and retrue the wheel, if necessary.

10. Check and retension the wheel every 50 km (30 miles) for the next 100 km (60 miles).

Rebuilding a Wheel

This is not a job for everyone—a professional can do it much faster. But it's wonderful therapy, and becomes easier as you do it more often. Before you start, take a very close look at the old wheel (or another similar wheel) and the various descriptions and drawings in this chapter that show spoking details—try to understand what's going on before you start.

Spoke-length Determination

Make sure you get the right spoke length—ask at the bike shop, telling them which hub and which rim you will be combining and which spoking pattern (radial, one-, two-, three-, or four-cross) you'll be using, and how many spokes will be used. Most modern lightweight wheels are built with 32 or even 28 spokes. On an off-set rear wheel (especially one used with a seven- or eight-speed freewheel block) the spokes on the RH side should be about 3 mm (⅛ in.) shorter than those on the LH side; or, if you can't find the optimum

Left: replacing the rim, with the new and the old rim taped together.

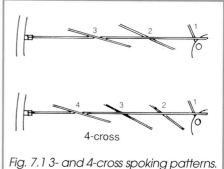

Fig. 7.1 3- and 4-cross spoking patterns.

spoke size, deviate a little on the low side for the spokes on the RH side, a little on the high side for the LH spokes.

If you have a programmable calculator, you can use the following formula to calculate the spoke length yourself (all dimensions in mm).

$$\text{Spoke length} = \sqrt{(A^2 + B^2 + C^2)} - 0.5\,S$$

where:

A = r sin (T)
B = R − r cos (T)
C = offset from outside hub flange to center of wheel (measured as shown in Detail A of Fig. 7.1) —on a front wheel, it is ½ the total hub width, on a rear wheel it will be different on both sides
r = ½ the effective hub diameter (measured as shown in detail B)
R = ½ the effective rim diameter (measured as shown in detail C)
T = 360 X/N
X = number of spoke crossings desired

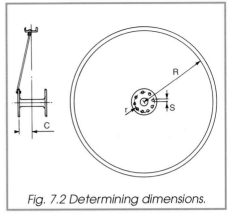

Fig. 7.2 Determining dimensions.

N = number of spokes per hub flange (usually, one half total number of spokes)
S = spoke hole diameter in hub flange

Spoke-length Check

You will be excused if you're scared off by the formula in the preceding section. Alternatively, here's a method of determining relatively painlessly whether you are using the correct spoke length, based on the principle that any plane is determined by three points. Use this method whenever you are not absolutely sure whether you have the correct spoke length.

No. of spokes in wheel	1-cross angle	1-cross spaces	2-cross angle	2-cross spaces	3-cross angle	3-cross spaces	4-cross angle	4-cross spaces	5-cross angle	5-cross spaces
24	75°	2½	135°	4½	–	–	–	–	–	–
28	64.3°	2½	115.7°	4½	167.1°	6½	–	–	–	–
32	56.3°	2½	101.3°	4½	146.3°	6½	–	–	–	–
36	50°	2½	90°	4½	130°	6½	170°	8½	–	–
40	45°	2½	81°	4½	117°	6½	153°	8½	–	–
44	40.9°	2½	73.6°	4½	106.4°	6½	139.1°	8½	171.8°	10½
48	37.5°	2½	67.5°	4½	97.5°	6½	127.5°	8½	157.5°	10½

Table 7-I Spoke hole spacing in hub for neighboring spokes in rim.

You'll need only six spokes—check whether they are all the same length first: hold them upright on the table, screwed ends down, and compare the height of the heads. If the spoke length is correct, continue spoking the entire wheel in the following manner.

Tools and equipment:

spoke wrench; medium screwdriver; lubricant (e.g. vaseline); cloth

Procedure:

1. Take six spokes and nipples; lubricate the spoke ends and wipe.

2. Hold the hub upright in front of you. On the upper hub flange, select three holes that are equally spaced (every sixth in the case of a 32-hole hub, which has 16 holes per flange; if the hub has more or less than 32 holes, you may not be able to space completely equally — just make sure the spokes are spaced as equally as possible, with an odd number of empty spoke holes in the flange between the spokes). If the hub has holes that are alternately countersunk ("beveled"), select holes that are beveled on the inside. Put a spoke through each of these holes from the outside through to the inside.

3. Inspect the spoke holes in the rim: take the hole next to the valve hole that is off-set up (on most rims sold in the U.S., that is the first hole going counterclockwise, but it may also be the first one going clockwise, especially on Italian rims). Attach one of the three spokes with the nipple in this hole. Mark it with adhesive tape—we'll call it spoke 1.

4. Count out the same number of holes that are offset upward as there are vacant holes in the hub, going the same direction (clockwise or counterclockwise). Place the other two spokes in the corresponding holes determined this way. Now the spokes in the upper hub flange should be connected to similarly spaced holes that are off-set upward in the rim—correct if necessary.

5. Turn the wheel over, so that the side without spokes faces up.

6. Visually line up the two hub flanges, noting how the holes in the near flange are positioned between the holes in the far

Wheel spoking using a truing stand.

flange. I'll call this offset from one hole in the one flange to the nearest hole in the other flange a "half space," while I'll call the space between consecutive holes in the same flange a "whole space."

7. To find the location for the first spoke inserted on the flange that is on top now, read off the number of spaces from the table, as a function of the number of spokes and the number of spoke crossings required (e.g. 6½ for a four-cross pattern with 32 spokes). Count the appropriate number of spaces from the hole where spoke 1 (marked with tape) is located in the direction of the valve hole (i.e. going counter-clockwise if the valve hole is counterclockwise from the spoke). In the hub flange hole thus established, insert a spoke from the outside to the inside, and attach this spoke to the free spoke hole in the rim immediately adjacent to the valve hole.

8. Count the same number of spoke holes in the hub on either side of this spoke as you count between corresponding spokes on the lower flange on either side of spoke 1, inserting the two remaining spokes there, again from the outside to the inside.

9. Attach these spokes to the rim in the holes that are in the same relative position to each other as the two spokes on either side of the valve hole.

10. Stop to check whether you've got something that looks like Fig. 7.3,

and if not, where you went wrong. Correct if necessary.

11. Tighten the six spokes gradually until the wheel is reasonably tight and centered (front wheel) or appropriately off-set ("dished" rear wheel) as required. If significant thread is exposed under the nipple (more than 1 thread), choose a longer spoke; if any part of the spoke protrudes beyond the nipple inside the rim, choose a shorter spoke — and start all over again. If the spoke length is correct, continue building the wheel more or less as described in the following procedure *Spoking Procedure*, starting at step 4.

Note:

If you are building a radially spoked (front) wheel, insert all spokes from the inside to the outside, so they all lie on the outside of the hub flanges.

Spoking procedure:

This instruction is based on the assumption that you have determined the correct spoke length.

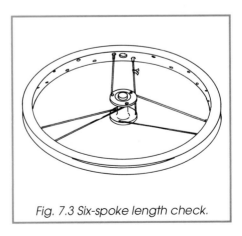

Fig. 7.3 Six-spoke length check.

If you're not sure, first carry out the check described above under *Spoke Length Check*, after which you'll be well on your way and can pick up the instructions starting at step 4. If you're rebuilding a wheel using an old hub or an old rim (or both), first cut away all the old spokes and remove them. If you're reusing the spokes and the hub, follow the earlier procedure *Replacing Rim*.

Tools and equipment:

spoke wrench; medium size screwdriver; lubricant (e.g. vaseline); cloth

Procedure:

1. Check whether all the spokes are the same length: take them all in your hand and push them ends-down on the table, and compare the heights of the heads. Lubricate the threaded ends and wipe off excess lubricant.

2. Take 8 spokes (assuming a 32-spoke wheel—more or less for other wheels), and put one through every second hole in one of the hub flanges from the outside to the inside. If holes are alternately countersunk on the inside and the outside of the hub flange, select those holes that are countersunk on the inside.

3. Putting the hub in front of you, held vertically with the batch of spokes stuck through the upper flange, find the spoke hole in the hub that's immediately next to the valve hole and is off-set upward. Take one spoke and attach it with the nipple to that

hole; mark this spoke (e.g. with tape). I'll refer to it as *spoke 1*. Screw on the nipple about five turns.

4. Similarly attach the other spokes so far installed in the hub into every fourth hole in the rim. If you followed the instruction *Spoke Length Check* above, just put in the remaining spokes—you already have three of them.

5. Check to make sure all these spokes are attached to spoke holes that are off-set upward in the rim, and that three free spoke holes remain between each pair of consecutive spokes in the rim, one free hole in the hub.

6. Turn the wheel over and establish whether the remaining free hole immediately next to the valve hole is oriented clockwise or counterclockwise. Select the spoke holes in the flange now nearest to you that are each off-set half a space from the spokes already installed on the far flange in that same direction. Insert the next set of 8 (or whatever is the appropriate number) spokes in these holes, leaving a free hole between each set of consecutive spokes.

7. Locate spoke 1 (the one on the far flange next to the valve hole) and count out the appropriate number of spaces to determine where the next spoke is, which you'll attach in the free spoke hole on the other side of the valve hole, counting clockwise if the free spoke hole is also clockwise from the valve hole, counterclockwise if the free

hole is counterclockwise from the valve hole. If you followed the instruction *Spoke Length Check* this has already been determined — just install the missing spokes.

8. Attach the remaining spokes so far inserted in the hub into every fourth spoke hole in the rim.

9. You should now have sets of two spokes, each set separated by two free holes in the rim and by one free hole in the hub flanges. Make any corrections that may be required.

10. Insert the next batch of spokes from the inside to the outside in one of the hub flanges.

11. Take any one of these spokes and "lace" it to cross the chosen number of spokes on the same hub flange for the crossing pattern selected, always crossing under the last one. If you're building a four-cross wheel, that will be over the first, over the second, over the third and then forced under the fourth. Attach this spoke in the next free hole in the rim that's offset in the corresponding direction. If it doesn't fit, you either have the wrong spoke length for the pattern selected, have tightened the other spokes too much (rarely the case), or you made a mistake somewhere along the line—check and restart if necessary.

12. Do the same with the last batch of spokes, inserting them in the free holes in the other hub flange from the inside to the outside, making the right crossings; then install

them in the remaining spoke holes in the rim.

13. You now have a complete but loosely spoked wheel. Once more, check to make sure the pattern is correct as you intended, then start tightening the spoke nipples progressively, working around several times, first using the screwdriver, then—when the nipples begin to get tighter— with the spoke wrench. Don't tighten too much though: it should remain easy to turn the nipples with the spoke wrench.

14. Check whether the wheel is correctly centered between the locknuts at the wheel axle, as outlined in step 3 of the description *Wheel Truing*, above, and the subsequent note.

One side done: waiting for the second set of spokes to be installed.

Wheel-dishing check.

15. Install the wheel in the bike, which should be hung up off the ground by saddle and handlebars or placed upside-down (taking care to support it at the handlebars so nothing gets damaged), and make the same kind of corrections as outlined under *Wheel Truing* above, until the wheel is perfectly round and has no lateral deflection.

16. Proceed to tighten the spokes all around equally. Unless you're an experienced piano tuner, it's hard to explain in writing how tight is right. Just compare with another good wheel (ask in the bike shop) to develop a feel for the right tension. Tension is checked by pushing spokes together in crossed pairs at a point between the rim and the last cross. On an off-set rear wheel, the RH spokes (i.e. those on the chain side) should be considerably tighter than those on the other side. All the spokes on the same side of a wheel must be equally tight.

17. Now take spokes together in sets of four—two nearby sets of crossing spokes on each side of the wheel—and squeeze them together quite forcefully. This will bend the spokes into their final shape and release all sorts of built-up stresses, resulting in some disturbing sounds. Don't be perturbed—if you don't do this now it will happen while you're riding the bike, when it's too late to make the required corrections.

18. After this stress-relieving operation, check the wheel for roundness and tightness once more—you will probably have to tighten several spokes a little more.

19. After perhaps 40 km (25 miles) of cycling, check and true the wheel once more. It's a lot of work, but think of the satisfaction.

Notes:

1. A radially spoked wheel (sometimes used for a front wheel) is simpler to spoke, since all spokes can be inserted from the inside to the outside, finishing up on the outside of the hub flanges of the finished wheel.

2. Nowadays, some manufacturers offer special hubs designed for radially spoked wheels with straight spokes. The parts must match.

CHAPTER 8

The Drivetrain

The drivetrain comprises the parts that transmit the rider's legwork to the rear wheel. On the road bike, they include the bottom bracket with cranks and chainrings, the pedals, the chain, and the freewheel with cogs. The derailleurs, which are sometimes considered part of the drive-train, are covered separately in Chapter 9, which is devoted to the derailleur gearing system.

The Cranks

All modern road bikes are equipped with aluminum cotterless cranks, while cottered models may be found on some old bikes. Cotterless cranks are held onto square tapered ends of the spindle by a matching square tapered hole and a bolt or nut, depending on the design of the spindle. Since those held with bolts are usually better than those held with nuts, choose the former when replacing a bottom bracket. Currently, some manufacturers use an Allen bolt that is accessible from outside.

Except in the case of the Allen-bolt type, the bolt or nut is covered by a dustcap, which protects the screw thread in the recess. This screw thread is used to pull the crank off the spindle for maintenance or replacement by means of a crank extractor tool. The RH crank has an attachment spider or ring, to which the chainrings are bolted.

The crank extractor consists of two parts, which may be permanently combined: a wrench for the crank bolt, and the actual extractor. Crank bolts come in sizes 14–16 mm; most quality bikes use 15 mm crank bolts.

The road bike's drivetrain. This one is equipped with Shimano Dura Ace components: crankset, pedals, front and rear derailleur, and chain.

The crank extractor fits into the threaded hole surrounding the crank bolt, and pulls the crank off its spindle when it is tightened. For the 22 mm threaded holes found on most bikes, I recommend the Campagnolo tool, which has a separate long-handled wrench. TA and Stronglight cranks have 23 mm threaded holes and require a specific tool. The types with an Allen bolt require only one Allen key (usually 6 or 7 mm).

A new bike's cranks should be tightened every 40 km (25 miles) for the first 200 km (125 miles), since initially the soft aluminum of the cranks deforms so much that the connection between the spindle and the crank tends to come loose. This is the reason you should carry the crank bolt wrench tool in your repair kit.

Using crank extractor tool to pull the crank off the spindle.

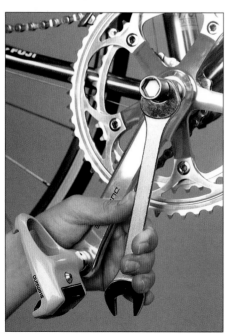

Beyond that, the crank is merely removed when it is damaged or when you have to adjust or overhaul the bottom bracket.

It is not uncommon in off-road cycling to bend a crank during a fall. Before you replace the entire crank, let a bike mechanic try to straighten it out. This requires a special tool that is not worth buying for the average home mechanic.

Replacing a Cotterless Crank

This job is necessary when a crank or an entire crankset has to be replaced. It also has to be done for many maintenance jobs on the bottom bracket.

Tools and equipment:

4–7 mm Allen wrench; adjustable pin wrench; crank extractor; crank bolt wrench; cloth; grease

Removal procedure:

1. Remove the dustcap, which can generally be done with a coin, though some models require the use of an Allen wrench or adjustable pin wrench. Some recent versions have Allen crank bolts with a flexible grommet, eliminating the need for a separate dustcap.

2. Unscrew the bolt or the nut with the wrench part of the crank tool, while holding the crank firmly.

3. Remove the washer that lies under the bolt or nut. This is an important step; if you forget to do this, you will not be able to

remove the crank, but will damage it.

4. Make sure the internal part of the crank extractor is retracted as far as it will go.

5. Dab a little grease on the crank extractor tool's threads, then screw it into the threaded recess in the crank by at least three full turns, preferably more.

6. Holding the crank with one hand to counter, turn the handle of the crank extractor (or the wrench that fits on it instead of a handle on some models). This will eventually pull the crank off the spindle.

7. Remove the tool from the crank.

Installation procedure:

1. Clean the matching surfaces of the spindle and the crank hole, then apply a thin layer of grease to these surfaces.

2. Push the crank onto the spindle, making sure the two cranks are 180° off-set and that the crank with the attachment for the chainrings goes on the RH side.

3. Install the washer.

4. Install the bolt or the nut and tighten it fully, then install the dust cap.

5. Firmly retighten the connection after about 40 km (25 miles).

Cottered Cranks

See Fig. 8.1 for this old, simple type of attachment. If the crank comes loose, tighten the nut. If the problem

persists (or to replace the crank), remove the nut and hammer out the cotter pin, while supporting the crank on something solid. When replacing the cotter pin, take the old one to the shop to make sure you get the right size.

Tools and equipment:

wrench to fit nut on cotter pin; hammer; something solid to support crank

Removal procedure:

1. Unscrew nut on cotter pin until the end of the cotter pin is about 1.5 mm (1/16 in.) below the top of the nut, or by at least two full turns, whichever is more.

2. Supporting the crank with something solid, hammer down the nut until it touches the crank.

3. Unscrew the nut completely and push or hammer the cotter pin out; remove the crank.

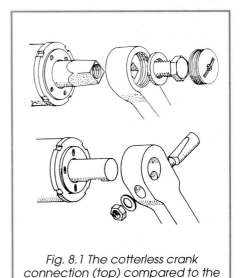

Fig. 8.1 The cotterless crank connection (top) compared to the old method with cotter pin (bottom).

Installation procedure:

1. Place the crank on the spindle. Note that the hole in the crank must be lined up with the groove in the spindle, and that the crank with the chainwheel or the attachment for the chainwheel is on the RH side (chain side) of the bike.

2. Place the cotter pin through the crank from the bigger hole (assuming one of the holes is bigger, which can easily be verified by trying to put the cotter pin in from both sides). The flat side of the cotter pin must be aligned with the groove in the spindle.

3. Supporting the crank with something solid, hammer the cotter pin in until enough screw thread protrudes to install the

Modern cartridge bearing. This type is installed as a complete unit, and requires a special tool.

washer and the nut, then tighten the nut fully; hammer down and tighten again.

Note:

If the cotter pin is damaged or if the thread is worn so much that the nut feels loose, it should be replaced by one of the same diameter (several different diameters are in use). By way of temporary repair, installing a second nut (locknut) may do the trick. Filing the flat face down until it is smooth will be sufficient if the cotter pin is not too seriously deformed. Tighten again after about 40 km (25 miles) of use. If for some reason the crank must be replaced, make sure to get one for the same spindle diameter and the same pedal-thread size (see instructions for pedal replacement elsewhere in this chapter).

The Bottom Bracket

This is the heart of the drivetrain, installed in the frame's bottom bracket shell. It is made up of the spindle, or axle, to which the cranks are attached, and the ball bearings that allow it to turn smoothly. The conventional, or BSA, type has adjustable bearings, whereas the bearings of the cartridge (or sealed) unit are not adjustable, although some models can be adjusted laterally to improve the chain line.

If a cartridge bottom bracket develops play or tightness, the bearing cartridges have to be replaced. Except for special models that are easily removable, you may have to take the bike to a shop to have it overhauled or replaced.

Adjusting Bottom Bracket

Carry out this work on a conventional bottom bracket when the bearings have developed play or when they are too tight.

Tools and equipment:

bottom bracket tools (special wrenches for the lockring and the bearing cups)

Procedure:

1. Unless it is a model with an adjustable cup with flats for use of a wrench, remove the LH crank.

2. Loosen the lockring on the LH side by about one half turn.

3. Loosen the adjustable bearing cup by turning it a quarter turn counterclockwise if the bearing is too tight, clockwise if it is too loose.

Left: checking bearing play at the bottom bracket.
Top right: loosening the lockring that holds the bottom bracket bearing.
Bottom right: adjusting the bearing using a pin wrench.

4. Restraining the bearing cup, tighten the lockring, then repeat to fine-tune the adjustment if necessary.

Notes:

1. Bottom bracket looseness is best detected with the cranks installed, using them for leverage while twisting sideways.

2. Tightness is best established when the cranks are removed.

3. If you can get the pin wrench for the adjustable cup ground down

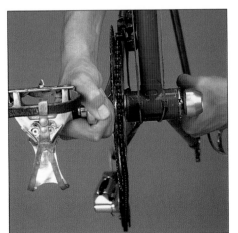

so it fits between the crank and the cup, is possible to carry out this adjustment without removing the LH crank.

Overhauling Bottom Bracket

This description applies to conventional bottom brackets. Cartridge-bearing bottom brackets vary from one model to the next and usually require special tools—refer any problems to the bike shop. Other models will be treated separately.

Tools and equipment:

crank bolt wrench; crank extractor; bottom bracket tools; cloths; solvent; bearing grease

Dismantling procedure:

1. Remove the LH and RH cranks.

2. Loosen and remove the lockring on the LH side.

3. Loosen and remove the adjustable bearing cup with the pin wrench (or, on older models, with a matching thin open-ended wrench), catching the bearing balls which are usually held in a retainer.

4. Pull the spindle out, also catching the bearing balls on the other side.

Top left: the bearing cup removed, exposing the ball bearings for lubrication.
Bottom left: removing the spindle.
Right: sealed bearing, as used on most modern bottom brackets.

Overhauling procedure:

1. Clean and inspect all parts, checking for corrosion, wear, and damage—grooved or pitted bearing surfaces.

2. If there is serious damage or wear, also check the condition of the fixed (RH) bearing cup, which otherwise remains on the bike. Except on some imported French and Italian bikes (which have RH thread), the fixed cup invariably has LH threading.

3. Replace any parts that are visibly corroded, damaged, or worn, taking the old parts to the shop with you to make sure you get matching replacements.

Installation procedure:

1. Pack both cleaned bearing cups with bearing grease.

2. If the fixed bearing cup has been removed, reinstall it, turning it counterclockwise.

3. Push the bearing ball retainers into the grease-filled bearing cups, making sure they are placed in such a way that only the balls—not the metal of the retainer—contact the cup.

4. Put the spindle in from the LH side —with the longer end (for the chainring side) first, if it is not symmetrical.

5. Install the adjustable cup with its bearing ball retainer in place.

6. Install the lockring.

7. Adjust the bearing as described in the preceding description until it runs smoothly and without play.

Lateral Adjustment of Cartridge Bottom Bracket

Although the bearings of these units usually cannot be adjusted to compensate for play or wear, at least the screw-threaded versions allow something that cannot easily be done with other bottom brackets: their lateral position relative to the centerline of the bike can be adjusted. This makes it relatively easy to correct the chain line (the alignment of chainring and cog, which will be covered below). You will need the special lockring wrenches for the unit in question. Just loosen the one lockring and tighten the other one until the bearing unit is moved over sideways into the desired position.

Chainring Maintenance

On any road bike, the chainrings are installed on the RH crank by one of several methods. Once a month, ascertain that the chainrings are still firmly in place by tightening the little bolts that hold them to each other and to the cranks, respectively.

Most chainrings are attached with 5 mm Allen bolts, though some models use slotted nuts on one side, for which a slotted screwdriver or hooked tool is used.

Worn chainrings will result in increased resistance and poor shifting. Replace them if they are obviously worn or when teeth are cracked.

If individual teeth are bent, they can sometimes be straightened. When the whole chainring is warped, it can be straightened by carefully using a wedge-shaped block of wood and pushing it between chainstay and chainring or between individual chainrings where they are too close. These jobs can both be done with the chainrings on the bike.

Replacing Chainring

This job is necessary when the chainrings are beyond repair or when you want to change to a different gearing range. First remove the crank, then undo the Allen bolts. The chainrings should not be reversed— remember to replace them facing the

Left: detail of road bike chainrings and RH crank unit.
Right: removing the bolts that hold the chainrings to the RH crank unit.

right direction. Chainrings with easy-shifting special tooth profiles, and off-round chainrings, such as the now virtually extinct Bio-Pace, have a marker that should be lined up with the crank arm for the correct orientation.

The Pedals

Most road bikes now come with clipless pedals, to which matching cycling shoes can be clipped. Older bikes may have regular pedals that are used in conjunction with toeclips and straps.

All pedals are screwed into the cranks with a normal RH threaded connection on the right, a LH one on the left. They are usually marked R and L, but if you are not certain which pedal goes in which crank arm, do check the threading first.

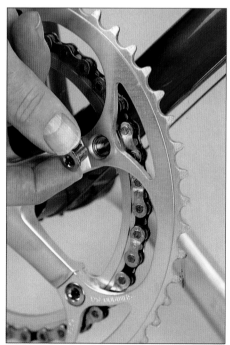

Pedal maintenance operations are limited to adjustment, overhauling and the replacement of a pedal.

Replacing Pedals

This job may also be necessary when transporting the bike on a plane or a bus. The description is equally valid for regular and clipless pedals.

Tools and equipment:

6 mm Allen wrench or pedal wrench; antiseize lubricant or grease

Removal procedure:

1. Restrain the crank firmly by straddling the bicycle and placing your foot on either pedal. Place the pedal wrench around the pedal spindle and unscrew the RH pedal counterclockwise, the LH pedal clockwise. Once one

Removing the pedal.
Left: using an Allen wrench from the back of the crank.
Right: using a pedal wrench from the front of the crank.

pedal is removed, restrain that crank arm as you remove the other pedal.

2. Unscrew the connection between the pedal and the crank. If the pedal has a hexagonal recess in the end of the threaded stub (reached from behind the crank), you may attempt to use the Allen wrench. If the pedal is tight, the Allen wrench may not give sufficient leverage, even if there is a hexagonal recess.

Installation procedure:

1. Clean the threaded hole in the crank and the threaded stub on the pedal, then put some antiseize or grease on both threaded parts.

2. Carefully align the screw thread and gently screw in the pedal by hand, turning the RH pedal clockwise, the LH pedal counterclockwise.

Notes:

1. If you remove the pedals frequently (e.g. if you travel by air with the bike a lot), place a

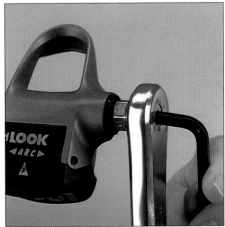

1–2 mm thin steel washer (again with some grease) between the face of the pedal stub and the face of the crank.

2.. When the pedal hole in the crank is worn out, it can be drilled out and a Helicoil insert installed, which provides new screw thread.

Adjusting Pedal Bearings

This description applies only to adjustable-bearing pedals. Most modern clipless models, and a few high-end conventional models, have sealed cartridge bearings that cannot be adjusted but must be replaced at a bike shop when they develop play or resistance.

Tools and equipment:

8–10 mm socket wrench; small screwdriver; dustcap tool, needle nose pliers, or 4–6 mm Allen wrench; grease; cloth

Procedure:

1. Remove the dustcap.

2. Loosen the locknut by one turn.

3. Lift the underlying keyed washer with the tip of the screwdriver to loosen it.

4. Using the screwdriver, turn the cone ¼ turn to the right (clockwise) to tighten the bearing, to the left (counterclockwise) to loosen it.

5. Restraining the cone with the screwdriver to make sure it does not turn, tighten the locknut. Add grease if the bearings are dry.

6. Check and readjust if necessary. There should be neither noticeable play nor tightness.

7. Reinstall the dustcap.

Left: conventional pedal bearing exposed for adjustment.
Right: conventional pedal disassembled for overhaul.

Overhauling Conventional Pedals

This is required if adjustment does not have the desired effect. Often the problem will be a bent spindle, and then—depending whether such parts are stocked for the model in question—you may have to replace the pedals altogether.

Tools and equipment:

dustcap tool; 8–10 mm socket wrench; small screwdriver; grease; cloth

Dismantling procedure:

1. Remove the dustcap, preferably using the special tool.

2. Loosen the locknut and remove it.

3. Lift the underlying keyed washer with the tip of the screwdriver to loosen it and then remove it.

4. Using the screwdriver, turn the cone to the left (counterclockwise) to loosen and remove it, catching the bearing balls with the rag placed underneath the pedal as you do so.

5. Pull the pedal housing off the spindle, also catching the bearing balls on the other side. Count and save all bearing balls. They are quite small and can be easily lost.

Overhauling procedure:

1. Clean and inspect all bearing surfaces and the pedal axle.

2. Replace anything that is damaged, corroded, grooved, or pitted, as well as the pedal spindle if it is bent—or the whole pedal if no spares are available.

3. To make sure you get the right parts when replacing pedal parts or bearing balls, take the old ones to the bike shop for comparison.

Reassembly procedure:

1. Fill both bearing cups with grease and push the bearing balls into this bed of grease, making sure there is just a little room between the balls—one bearing ball less than the maximum.

2. Put the pedal housing on the spindle with the larger side (the end without the dustcap screw threading) first—towards the crank.

3. After you've made sure you have not lost any bearing balls, install the adjustable cone.

4. Install the keyed washer with the key fitting in the groove in the pedal spindle.

5. Install the locknut, restraining the cone so it does not turn with it.

6. Adjust the bearing as described above.

7. Install the dustcap.

Cartridge-Bearing Pedals

Clipless pedals, and other models running on cartridge bearings are not adjustable. The most important maintenance operation is exterior cleaning with water and a fine brush. The clipless pedal can be replaced following the same instructions that apply to ordinary pedals. To lubricate or replace the bearings, first remove the bearing cartridge with the manufacturer's special tool. Pack the cartridge bearings with grease.

The Chain

All modern road bikes (in fact all derailleur bikes) are equipped with a narrow $3/32$ x$1/2$ in. chain without a special connecting clip link. The life expectancy of a road bike chain is about a year—but less if you ride in bad weather.

Clean and lubricate the chain as described in the section *Preventive Maintenance* in Chapter 4, depending on the kind of weather and terrain you ride in. From time to time, remove the chain to rinse it out in a solvent with 5–10% motor oil mixed in, and then lubricate it thoroughly. In the following section, we shall cover removal and installation of the chain.

Left: removing the bearing-and-spindle unit from a cartridge bearing pedal.
Right: adjusting the tension on a clipless pedal.

Sometimes, shifting problems will occur after the bike has been in a spill, due to a twisted chain. This may happen when the derailleur was twisted, trapping the chain in place. Check for this and replace the chain if it is twisted.

When selecting a new chain, make sure you get one that is particularly narrow if your bike has seven or eight cogs in the back.

Replacing Chain

The work described here has to be done whenever you replace or remove the chain for a thorough cleaning job. Also, some derailleur maintenance operations are best done with the chain removed from the bike. Special chains that are designed for smoother shifting, matching the same manufacturer's tooth shape on its chainrings and cogs, may require

special attention. Although to date mainly used on mountain bikes, they are showing up on some road bikes. Use the special chainlink pin and use only the special chaintool designed for the model in question.

Tools and equipment:

chain rivet extractor; cloths

Removal procedure:

1. With the aid of the derailleurs, and while turning the cranks with the rear wheel lifted off the ground, put the chain onto the small chainring in the front and one of the smallest cogs at the back.

2. Put the chain rivet extractor on one of the pins between two links with the punch firmly up against the chain link pin. Retract the handle of the chain rivet extractor and place the chain in the slot farthest from the handle.

3. Turn the handle by 6 turns, pushing the pin towards the opposite side.

4. Turn the handle back until the tool can be removed.

5. Try to separate the chain at this point, twisting it sideways. If that does not work, reinstall the tool and give it another turn until the chain comes apart. Make sure the pin does not come out altogether —if it does, replace the set of inner and outer links at the end.

Installation procedure:

1. Make sure the derailleurs are set for the small chainring in the

front and the second smallest or smallest cog at the back.

2. Wrap the chain around the chainring, cog, and derailleur, also passing through the front derailleur cage.

3. Routed this way, there should be just a little spring tension in the rear derailleur, tending to pull the chain tighter.

4. If the chain is too long, remove the links in sets of two—an outside link and the link within. Save these for spares.

5. Using the chain rivet extractor from the side where the pin protrudes, push it back in until it projects equally on both sides.

6. Twist the chain sideways a few times until it has come loose enough at this point to bend as freely as at the other links. If this can't be done, put the tool on the

Pushing out a pin to split the chain.

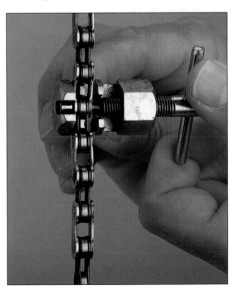

chain in the other slot closest to the handle and turn the handle against the pin just a little until the links are freed.

Note:

If you should accidentally push the pin out all the way when disassembling, install a section of two new links instead, after removing two more links—taking care not to lose the pin this time. Use a section of the same make and type of chain.

Chain Line

Ideally, the chain should run parallel to a line through the center of the bike's frame and wheels. On derailleur bikes, this means that the point in the middle of the chainrings should be in line with the middle of the freewheel block. On non-derailleur bikes, the chainring should be in line with the cog. To achieve that, it may be possible to adjust the bottom bracket cups sideways on a derailleur bike. Use a differently shaped cog on a bike without derailleurs. Sometimes a parallel line can only be achieved by straightening the frame (if the problem is due to misalignment).

The Freewheel

Nowadays, almost all manufacturers use a cassette unit, on which the freewheel cartridge with seven or eight cogs (also called sprockets) is

Left: twisting the chain to separate it at the pin.
Below: chain line. Note how the alignment of chainring and cog is not perfect in this photo, and it gets more extreme as you move to a higher or lower gear from this position.

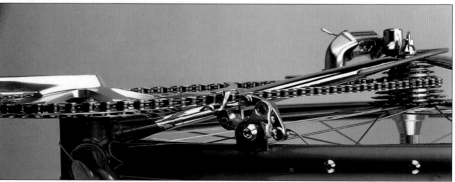

held with splines on the freewheel mechanism that is attached to the RH side of the hub. On older bikes, the freewheel mechanism is a unit containing the cogs and itself screwed onto screw thread on the RH side of the rear hub.

On cassette models, the freewheel cassette, or body, is held on the hub with a large internal hollow Allen bolt, while the cogs are installed on splines and locked in place by means of a threaded ring or a threaded smallest cog. I shall not go into any detail about the workings of the freewheel mechanism. If it doesn't work, get a new one (or a new freewheel cassette, in the case of the cassette hub). What is more important is knowing how to lubricate the mechanism, how to exchange cogs, and how to remove a complete freewheel block or cassette. Those are the subjects that will be covered here.

Freewheel Lubrication

Do this job if the freewheel block is running roughly, yet is not so old that it seems reasonable to replace it—I suggest once a year. For cassette-type freewheels, first remove the wheel axle and wheel bearings, starting from the RH side, then use a special tool called Freehub-Buddy that is screwed into the end of the cassette body to squirt in the lubricant.

Tools and equipment:

SAE 40 or thicker oil; old can or similar receptacle; brush; cloth

Procedure:

1. Before you lubricate the mechanism, clean the cogs, the spaces between them, and the visible end of the freewheel block, preferably with the wheel removed from the bike. This can be done using an old rag or stiff brush.

2. On freewheel blocks with an oil hole, add oil until it oozes out at the other end.

3. On freewheel blocks without an oil hole, put the wheel on its side with the freewheel block facing up, and a receptacle under the

This tool, the Freewheel Buddy, allows lubricating the cassette freewheel once you remove the rear wheel axle. Grease can be injected through it with a standard grease gun.

hub to catch excess oil. Turn the hub relative to the wheel, and introduce oil into the gap that is visible between stationary and turning parts of the freewheel block mechanism—until it comes out clean on the other side.

4. Let it drip until no more oil comes out, then clean off excess oil.

Replacing Screwed-on Freewheel Blocks

Not many bikes use this type these days, but you may encounter an old one, so you need to know how to go about it. Once the wheel is removed from the bicycle, you can usually tell a freewheel block from a freewheel cassette, because the former have internal splines or notches into which a freewheel tool fits.

Tools and equipment:

freewheel tool; vise or 10-inch crescent wrench; grease; cloth

Removal procedure:

1. Remove the rear wheel from the bike.

2. Remove the quick-release or the axle nut and its washer on the RH side.

3. Place the freewheel tool on the freewheel block with the ribs or prongs on the tool exactly matching the splines or notches in the freewheel body.

4. Install the quick-release or the RH axle nut, leaving 2 mm (3/32 in.) space.

5. If you have a vise available, clamp the tool in with the side matching the freewheel facing up; if not, place the wrench on the flat faces of the tool and clamp the

Left: conventional screwed-on freewheel (on solid-axle tandem hub). Right: removing a conventional screwed-on freewheel block using a freewheel tool and a wrench.

wheel securely, with the tire pushed against the floor and one wall of the room. Be careful when using SunTour removers to avoid breaking off their fragile prongs.

6. To loosen the screw thread between hub and freewheel, forcefully turn either the wheel relative to the vise, or the wrench relative to the wheel about one turn counterclockwise, until the space between the tool and the nut is taken up.

7. Loosen the nut another two turns and repeat this process until the freewheel can be removed by hand, holding the tool.

To remove the entire cassette with freewheel mechanism, remove the hub axle from the LH side, and then loosen the internal hollow Allen bolt from the RH side.

Installation procedure:

1. Clean the threaded surfaces of the freewheel block (inside) and the hub (outside), and coat these surfaces with grease to prevent corrosion and to ease subsequent removal.

2. Put the wheel down horizontally with the threaded end facing up.

3. Carefully screw the freewheel block on by hand, making sure that it is correctly threaded on, until it cannot be tightened further.

4. Install the wheel, and allow the driving force to tighten it as you ride.

Replacing the Cassette Freewheel

If no internal notches or splines to take a tool are visible, you probably have a cassette-type freewheel. It is held inside the rear hub with an internal Allen bolt.

Tools and equipment:

9 or 10 mm Allen wrench

Removal procedure:

1. Dismantle the hub bearing on the LH side, and remove the axle.

2. Hold the wheel firmly and unscrew the freewheel cassette (with its cogs) with the big Allen key (10 mm for Shimano, 9 mm for Campagnolo).

Installation procedure:

1. Carefully clean and very lightly lubricate the thread of the freewheel cassette and the hole in the hub.

2. Accurately place the freewheel cassette (with its cogs) in the hub.

3. Tighten the freewheel cassette with the big Allen key.

Note:

If the wheel locks up, it is probably because the internal Allen bolt is not tightened down fully. To correct this problem, remove the RH locknut and cone, then pull the axle from the LH side and tighten the freewheel cassette with the 9 or 10 mm Allen wrench. Then reassemble.

To disassemble the packet of cogs on a cassette freewheel, remove the top ring or the smallest cog.

Replacing Cogs on the Cassette Freewheel

On these units, the cogs are held in splines on the freewheel cassette, held together with a lockring (Shimano) or a screwed-on smallest cog (Campagnolo).

Usually, one of the splines is wider, to ensure correct alignment of the teeth of subsequent cogs, so make sure you orient and line the cogs up up properly.

Tools and equipment:

2 chain whips, or sometimes only one and a special tool to fit lockring; freewheel tool; 10-inch crescent wrench

Dismantling procedure:

1. Remove the wheel from the bike.

2. Place the wheel horizontally in front of you with the freewheel cassette facing up.

The cogs taken off the splined cassette freewheel body.

3. On Shimano Hyperglide models, originally developed for mountain bike use but now also found on some road bikes, use the chain whip to restrain the largest cog while using the freewheel tool to unscrew the locking cog. Other freewheel cassettes can be removed with two chain whips by simply turning the last (smallest) cog against the biggest one.

4. Remove the cogs and the spacers, noting the sequence of the various cogs and spacers.

Installation procedure:

1. Install the cogs and the spacers in the same sequence.

2. Screw on the last cog or the notched ring, while countering with a chain whip wrapped around one of the other cogs.

Replacing Cogs on the Screwed-on Freewheel Block

On these conventional units, most or all of the cogs are screwed onto the freewheel. The procedure is similar to that outlined for the cassette freewheel, except that you will always need two chain whips, one wrapped around the smallest cog, one around one of the other ones. When you have finished reassembly, put the chain on the smallest cog and stand on the pedals to tighten it. Readjust the derailleur, if necessary.

Minor Freewheel Overhaul

Do this work to eliminate the wobbling effect of an obviously loose freewheel mechanism. It also may be worthwhile in other cases of freewheel trouble, since you may solve the problem without having to replace the freewheel.

Left: using two chain whips to remove a cog.
Right: using a chain whip together with a freewheel tool.

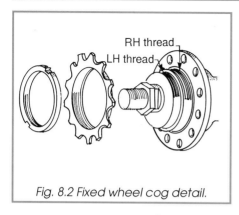

RH thread

LH thread

Fig. 8.2 Fixed wheel cog detail.

First, remove the rear wheel from the bike, but leave the freewheel on the hub. Clean the outside of the freewheel (also between the cogs) before commencing. Although the description assumes a conventional screwed-on freewheel, the same work can be done on a cassette-type freewheel. In that case, first remove the wheel axle by undoing the LH side bearing.

Tools and equipment:

special pin wrench (or a drift and a hammer); rag; bearing grease; 30–45 cm (12–15 in.) piece of twine

Procedure:

1. Using the pin wrench or, in a pinch, hammer and drift, unscrew the freewheel bearing cone, by turning to the right.

2. Remove the shim (or one of several shims) installed under the

cone. This reduces the gap between the two bearing races and usually solves the problem.

Note:

If you had another problem, proceed with disassembling the mechanism to establish whether it can be corrected. Embed the bearing balls in a generous layer of bearing grease.

3. Reinstall the freewheel bearing cone by screwing to the left and tightening firmly; then check whether it is operating smoothly now. If necessary, remove another shim or replace it with one of another thickness.

Fixed-Wheel Bikes

Some people ride a road bike without derailleurs for training purposes. These bikes are equipped with a fixed wheel, i.e. they have a cog without a freewheel mechanism, as found on track-racing bikes. On these, the special hub has a shorter 2-part threaded stub. First the cog is screwed on with regular RH thread, then it is held in place by a lockring with LH thread.

You can remove the cog, e.g. to replace it with a bigger or smaller one for a better gear ratio, with a special lockring wrench. Just keep in mind that it has LH threading.

CHAPTER 9

The Gearing System

All regular road bikes are equipped with derailleur gears. The derailleur system comprises a front derailleur, also called a *changer* in the U.K., and a rear derailleur, sometimes referred to as a *gear mechanism* or simply *mech* in Britain. Both are operated by means of shift levers that are mounted either in combination with the brake levers on the handlebars or on the downtube. The shifters are connected to the derailleurs by means of flexible control cables. The rear derailleur moves the chain sideways from one cog, or sprocket, to another on the rear wheel-mounted freewheel, while the front derailleur moves the chain sideways from one chainring to the other.

Derailleur System Overview

Since the various cogs and chainrings have different numbers of teeth, varying the combination achieves a lower or higher gear. A low gear is achieved by selecting a small chainring in the front and a large cog in the rear. A high gear results when a large chainring is combined with a small cog.

Essentially all derailleur bikes sold since 1986 come equipped with indexed gearing. That means that

Overview of the derailleur system: front and rear derailleurs, used to move the chain from one combination of chainring and sprocket to another. Not shown here are the controls, which are usually combined with the brake levers on the handlebars, although some riders still prefer to use levers mounted on the frame's downtube.

there are distinct stops on the shift levers for each of the gears, eliminating the need for sensitive adjustments when shifting. For road bikes, several manufacturers have introduced gear shifters integrated in the brake levers. By and large, these systems are maintained and adjusted just like any other indexed derailleur system. The integrated brake-and-gear levers are one unit, so you'll have to replace the entire lever unit if either the brake lever or the gear shifter is damaged beyond repair. In general, although it is possible to get your gears to work with almost any combination of components, your chances are best if all the bits and pieces are from the same manufacturer and model series.

Adjusting the rear derailleur's shifting range at the set-stop screws.

This chapter describes all maintenance operations necessary to maintain and adjust the gearing system and its individual components.

Adjusting Derailleur Range

The most frequently occurring derailleur problem requiring maintenance is that one of the derailleurs either exceeds its full range or fails to reach it. Another common problem occurs when indexed shifting doesn't work properly, and the chain gets stuck between the chainrings or cogs.

Tools and equipment:

small screwdriver; cloth

Procedure:

1. Establish the nature of your problem:
    ☐ front or rear derailleur?
    ☐ too far or not far enough?
    ☐ left or right?

2. If necessary, put the chain back on the chainring or the cog, operating the shift lever to position the derailleur.

3. Observe how each derailleur is equipped with two set-stop screws, usually equipped with a little spring under the head, and usually marked with an H and an L for high and low gear, respectively.

4. Tightening one of these screws limits the range of the derailleur in the appropriate direction, while loosening the screw extends it.

5. If the chain came off on the RH side (outside, or high gear) on the front, tighten the screw marked H of the front derailleur by perhaps one turn. If it did not quite reach the last gear on that side, loosen the screw by about that much.

6. Check all the gears, turning the cranks with the rear wheel lifted off the ground. Readjust as necessary.

Note:
If the problem persists, adjust the relevant derailleur system completely, as described for front and rear derailleurs separately below.

The Rear Derailleur

Indexed mechanisms are almost always used on modern bikes, and generally set up to select one of 7 or 8 cogs (only 5 or 6 on older models). The RH shifter has a ratchet device that corresponds with specific settings of the rear derailleur, which in turn correspond with the positions of the individual cogs.

In the case of downtube shifters, there is usually a small selection lever to switch from the indexed mode to the so-called friction mode (actually just a finer ratchet), which allows the selection of intermediate positions. This is essential when the mechanism is no longer adjusted properly, allowing the selection of the right gear, especially for people who are not familiar with making derailleur adjustments. By the roadside, this will be your quick solution to any gearing problems that develop, since exact adjustment is more easily carried out

at home. The index and friction modes are usually identified by the letters I and F, respectively, marked on the shifter.

On bikes with integrated shifters operated from the brake levers, there is no such quick solution because such shifters don't allow for disengaging the index function.

Adjusting Rear Derailleur

Most gearing problems can be eliminated by some form of derailleur adjustment.

Tools and equipment:

small screwdriver; 5 mm Allen wrench; 8 mm wrench

Procedure:

1. To get by until you have time to do a more thorough adjusting job,

Adjusting the cable tension at the barrel adjuster for the rear derailleur.

select the friction mode on the RH shifter if you have downtube or over-the-bar shifters.

2. Adjust the cable tension, using the built-in adjusting barrel.

3. Shift the rear derailleur to the highest gear (smallest cog) while holding the bike's rear wheel off the ground. Shift the front derailleur to the largest chainring. Use your hand to turn the cranks to engage the chain in that gear (or the closest one to it).

4. Tighten or loosen the barrel to either release or increase tension on the cable. If the cable is too loose, you will notice this now.

5. If the range of the adjusting barrel is inadequate, the cable must be clamped in at a different point. Screw in the adjusting barrel all

You may have to clamp the cable in at a different point if the adjusting range of the barrel adjuster is not adequate.

the way, loosen the eye bolt or clamp nut that holds the cable at the derailleur, pull the cable from the end until it is taut but not under tension, and tighten the clamp nut or eye bolt again.

6. Try out all the gears and readjust the range if necessary, following the description above.

7. Now the derailleur operates correctly in friction mode. The next step will be to fine-tune the indexing. To do that, first with the shifter still set in the friction mode, select the lowest gear (biggest cog in the rear, combined with small chainring in the front) and make sure it achieves this gear correctly.

8. Select the highest gear again (largest chainring, smallest cog), then put the shifter in index mode, marked with the letter I.

9. Adjust the cable tension until the chain runs smoothly without scraping against the derailleur cage or the next-larger cog.

10. Move the shifter one notch for the next lower gear in the back, engaging the second smallest cog if it is adjusted correctly.

11. If the derailleur does not move the chain to the next cog, tighten the cable by about one half revolution of the adjusting barrel.

12. If the derailleur shifts past this second smallest cog, loosen the cable tension with the adjusting barrel by about half a turn.

13. Repeat steps 10 through 12 until the mechanism works smoothly in these two gears.

14. With the derailleur set for the second smallest cog, tighten the cable with the adjusting barrel just so far that the chain runs noisily, scraping against the third smallest cog.

15. Loosen the cable tension just so far that the noises are subdued, to achieve the optimal setting.

16. Ride the bicycle and attempt to shift all gears to verify correct adjustments.

Notes:

If adjusting does not solve the problem, first replace the cable and outer cable. Sometimes simply filing the newly cut outer cable end will solve your problems.

Most rear derailleurs have a third adjusting screw, with which the angle of the mechanism can be varied. Select the gear in which the chain runs on the biggest cog, and adjust it so that the chain comes close to it, without the cog scraping the pulley.

Overhauling Rear Derailleur

This work will be necessary when so much dirt has built up that operation of the mechanism has become unreliable and cannot be solved by adjusting.

Tools and equipment:

3 mm Allen wrench; 7 mm open-ended wrench; 2 small crescent wrenches; solvent; cloths; grease and spray lubricant

Procedure:

1. Remove the bolts at the little wheels, called the tension and jockey pulley, respectively, over which the chain runs, catching the wheels, bushings, and bolts.

2. Clean the wheels and the bushings inside, as well as all other parts of the mechanism that are more easily accessible now.

3. If the pulleys appear to be worn, take them to a bike shop and buy new ones. Although they look similar, they do differ—on many models the tension pulley even differs from the jockey pulley—so exact replacements are necessary.

4. If the cage is bent, carefully straighten it using two crescent

Opening up the rear derailleur's cage to replace the pulleys (jocky and tension wheels).

wrenches—one on either side of the bend. Continue dismantling only if the mechanism cannot be cleaned adequately without doing so. Before removing the hinged cage, visualize how the internal spring works, so you will be able to reinstall it correctly. If necessary, you can increase the spring tension by placing the end in a different notch.

5. Lubricate the bushings in the pulleys with grease, and all pivots with light spraycan oil.

6. Reassemble the chain cage with the pulley, guiding the chain through the cage.

7. Try out all the gears and adjust the derailleur if necessary.

Replacing Rear Derailleur

This is done when you overhaul the bike completely and when the derailleur must be replaced because its operation cannot be restored by adjusting or replacing parts.

Tools and equipment:

chain rivet extractor; 5 mm Allen key; small screwdriver; rag; grease

Removal procedure:

1. If you prefer to leave the chain intact, open up the cage by removing the bolt of the jockey pulley.

2. Otherwise, separate the chain using the chain rivet tool.

3. Cut the cable crimp, undo the cable attachment and catch the ferrules and cable housing.

4. Undo the derailleur attachment bolt and remove the derailleur.

Installation procedure:

1. When buying a new derailleur, make sure that it is compatible with the shifter and the freewheel block installed on the bike. For example, if you have a 7- or 8-speed shifter, you need a derailleur with enough travel for that distance.

2. Clean and grease the derailleur eye threads, and gently screw in the derailleur. Put the new derailleur in the same position as the old one, checking to make sure it pivots freely around the mounting bolt.

3. Attach the cable.

4. Either install the chain (if it had been removed) or open up the cage by removing the bolt of the jockey pulley to put the chain in place, then reinstall the guide wheel.

5. Try out all the gears and adjust the derailleur and the cable tension if necessary.

The Front Derailleur

Since road bikes are universally equipped with only 2 chainrings, there is no real need for indexing in the front.

The major maintenance work on the front derailleur is the range-adjusting procedure described above. In addition, cable tension can be adjusted following the same procedure as for the rear derailleur. Most front derailleurs used for road bikes do not have a cable adjuster built into the outer cable. In that case, any adjustments have to be made by repositioning the clamp on the inner cable.

Adjusting Front Derailleur

This job must be done when the front derailleur "dumps" the chain by the side of the chainrings or when one chainring cannot be reached, or when the chain scrapes on the derailleur cage.

Tools and equipment:

5 and 6 mm Allen wrench; small screwdriver

Procedure:

1. First make sure the derailleur cage is perfectly parallel to the chainring—loosen the attachment bolt and twist the derailleur into position before retightening if necessary.

2. Carry out any necessary adjustment of the set-stop screws.

3. Set the shifter in the position for the highest gear with the chain on the large outside chainring.

4. In this position, the cable should be just taut, though not under tension.

5. If necessary, tighten or loosen it by clamping the cable in at a

different point: loosen the eye bolt or clamp nut with either the 5 mm Allen key or 8 mm wrench, pull the cable taut, and tighten the eye bolt or clamp nut again.

6. Check all gears and make any other adjustments that may be necessary.

Replacing Front Derailleur

This may become necessary if the mechanism is bent or damaged— usually the result of a fall.

Tools and equipment:

5 or 6 mm Allen key; small screwdriver; chain rivet extractor

Removal procedure:

1. Loosen the cable attachment by unscrewing the eye bolt or the

On most modern road bikes, the front derailleur is bolted to a lug attached to the frame's seat tube, as shown here. Sometimes, it has a clamp with which it is held around the seat tube, especially on older bikes.

clamp nut, and pull the cable end out.

2. Either remove the chain with the chain rivet extractor or, on many models, you can open up the derailleur's chain guide cage by removing the little bolt through the bushing that connects the two sides in the back of the cage.

3. Undo the attachment bolt.

Installation procedure:

1. Install the derailleur on the seat tube, with the cage parallel to the chainrings. Don't tighten it solidly yet.

2. Fine-tune the position, leaving a distance of 2–4 mm (³⁄₃₂–³⁄₁₆ in.) clearance between the largest chainring and the bottom of the cage, making sure it is aligned.

Modern gear operation with integral shift-and-brake lever, pulled in to reveal the cables.

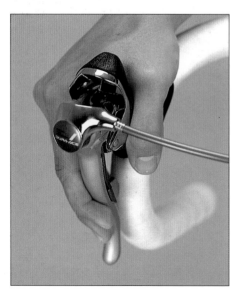

Now tighten the attachment bolt fully.

3. Feed the cable through the mechanism, and attach it in the eye bolt or under the clamp nut.

4. Adjust the cable tension so that it is just taut, but not under tension, with the shifter set for the highest gear and the chain on the largest chainring.

5. Check all the gears and adjust the derailleur range if necessary.

The Shifters

Whatever the shifter type, if it does not give satisfactory service, as evidenced by the derailleur's jumping out of the selected gear, the reason may be a damaged or corroded derailleur cable. So first check it, and replace cable and outer cable if necessary.

If the cable and the derailleur themselves are working properly, the problem may be due to either insufficient tension on the spring inside the mechanism, dirt or corrosion, or wear of the notched ring inside. Only in the latter case will it be necessary to replace the shifter.

First try cleaning and tensioning the shifter. Do not attempt to take your shifter apart unless it is a friction shifter. If it is, you can take it apart carefully and note where the various bits and pieces go. Then clean and lightly lubricate all parts with grease. Finally reassemble and if necessary turn the screw that holds it all together a little tighter.

Replacing Downtube Shifter

Here, we'll only talk about conventional downtube shifters. If the downtube shifter cannot be made to work by means of adjustment and cable replacement, it can easily be replaced.

Tools and equipment:

5 mm Allen key; small screwdriver; 8 mm wrench

Removal procedure:

1. Undo the inner cable clamp at the derailleur.

2. Remove the shifter attachment screw.

3. Pull the inner cable out and catch the cable casing and any loose items.

Installation procedure:

1. Attach the shifter in the desired location.

2. Feed the cable through the shifter with the nipple in the recess.

3. Guide the cable through the various guides and the cable casing, and attach the end at the derailleur.

4. Adjust the derailleur cable tension as described separately for front and rear derailleurs above.

Note on integrated lvers:

In the Shimano STI and Campagnolo Ergopower systems (the latter also sold under the Sachs brand name), the shifters are combined with the brake levers. They are installed, removed, and replaced together with the brake levers and you can follow the instruction, for bar-end shifters.

Left: bar-end shifter installation.
Ribht: downtube shifter installation.

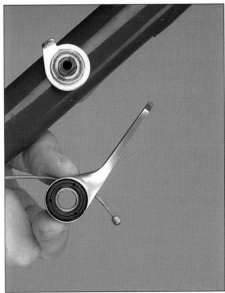

Replacing Bar-End Shifters

This type of shift lever requires special attention when installing, and the same procedure can be followed for SIS and other units with integrated shifting and braking controls. There are two basic types: with the cable routed through the handlebars or the cable routed outside the handlebars. The former require holes drilled in the handlebars, for which reason (or rather the resulting loss of strength) I would advise you to steer clear of them. If your handlebars have the holes pre-drilled, you may use that type, but I'd certainly advise you to get a model for external cable routing, rather than drill your own holes.

Tools and equipment:

wrenches to fit cable clamp bolt at derailleur and locknut on lever pivot bolt; pliers; medium screwdriver; Allen wrench for internal mounting bolt; lubricant

Disassembly procedure:

1. Place bike in the gear corresponding to the normal position for both derailleurs (always small cog in the rear, usually small chainwheel in the front).

2. Loosen the cable at the derailleur and free it from the guides and sections of inner cable as far as possible.

3. Unscrew the lever pivot bolt and remove the bushing and the locknut on the other side.

4. Remove the lever with the two washers, then remove the inner cable.

5. With the Allen wrench, loosen the internal mounting bolt, turning to the right; this will loosen the expander plug that holds the lever assembly mounting body in the end of the handlebars.

6. Now remove the inner cable (if run through the handlebars); remove the handlebar tape and outer cable in case you want to replace it and it is run outside the handlebars.

Installation procedure:

1. If the cable is to be run outside the handlebars, old handlebar tape and the old outer cable may have to be removed first.

2. Check to make sure the chain is in the gear that corresponds to the normal position for both derailleurs (small cog in the rear, usually small chainwheel in the front).

3. Route the outer cable along the handlebar so that it interferes as little as possible, but always at the bottom near the end where the lever is to be installed; attach with short pieces of adhesive tape (or run the cables through the handlebars if these have holes).

4. Wrap handlebar tape around the handlebars, as outlined in Chapter 11.

5. Loosely assemble the control body without the lever (i.e. expander plug, mounting bolt, and mounting body), with the

slot for the lever in line with the outer cable facing down. Tighten the mounting bolt by turning it to the left with the Allen key.

6. Slightly lubricate the lever bushing and contact surfaces, then install the lever, placing washers on either side. Tighten the pivot screw and the locknut.

7. Lubricate the inner cable, then thread it through the lever in such a way that the nipple will lie in the recess in the lever; now push the cable through the outer cable, over the guides, and attach to the derailleur. Alternately, you may prefer to thread the inner cable through the lever and the outer cable before installing the lever in the mounting unit—it always must be done this way when the cable is run through the handlebars.

8. Place the lever in the horizontal position and pull the cable taut with the pliers at the derailleur, then attach firmly. Make any adjustments as described for the front and rear derailleurs elsewhere in this chapter.

Twistgrip Shifters

These devices are mainly used on triathlon bikes, because they are easily accessible from their forward-pointing handlebar extensions. In addition to the original manufacturer, GripShift, several other types are available and they all work just fine with any Shimano derailleur.

Installation Procedure:

1. Follow the instructions for cable removal above, and then remove the old shifter and the handgrip.

2. Hook the cable nipple in the recess and route the cable through from inside, keeping the outer cable in place.

3. Install the twistgrip like any other handgrip, but tighten it with the clamping screw when it is in such a position that the numbers are visible from the rider's position.

4. Route the cable to the derailleur and clamp it in, keeping the outer cable taut.

5. Put the twistgrip shifter in the position for the highest gear and clamp in the end. Adjust the derailleur until the cable is taut.

6. Adjust the cable tension until all the gears work properly.

Derailleur Cables

For indexed shifters, relatively stiff stainless steel inner cables and a nylon sleeve between inner cable and outer cable were introduced. These same cables can also be used on non-indexed systems. They only need to be cleaned from time to time and checked to make sure they are not pinched or damaged anywhere.

Other cables (without the nylon sleeve) must also be lubricated from time to time. This is best done by removing them and smearing grease over the inner cable. Alternatively, squirt a few drops of oil between the inner cable and the cable casing at the

On some bikes, there is a derailleur cable tensioning device like this installed. Don't forget to tighten it before doing your final adjustment.

ends where the inner cable disappears into the casing.

Replacing Derailleur Cable

This work is necessary if the cable is pinched or otherwise damaged, or if the inner cable shows signs of corrosion or frayed strands. If you have under-the-bar shifters, the cable must match the shifter, since some manufacturers use different nipples.

Tools and equipment:

5 mm Allen wrench; 8 mm wrench; cable cutters ; screwdriver; file

Removal procedure:

1. Undo the cable at the derailleur by loosening the cable clamp nut

or the eye bolt that holds the cable to the derailleur.

2. Put the shifter in the position for the highest gear.

3. On under-the-bar shifters, open up the mechanism only to the point where the cable and the nipple are exposed.

4. Push the cable free at the shifter.

5. Pull the cable out and catch the outer cable and any other loose items such as cable end caps and ferrules.

Installation procedure:

1. Grease the cable, and file the outer cable ends if it is a replacement.

2. Feed the cable through the shifter as shown, with the nipple in the recess. If there is a nipple at each end, cut off the one that you won't use.

3. Guide the inner cable through the various guides and stops on the frame and the cable casing, then thread it through the derailleur clamp. Apply gentle torque once correct tension is established.

4. After you have established the correct cable length and have adjusted the tension, crimp or solder the strands of the inner cable end together to prevent fraying.

CHAPTER 10

The Brakes

All road bikes come with a type of rim brakes referred to as caliper brakes, and almost universally of the type called sidepull brakes. The principle is that two brake pads are pushed against the sides of the rim. Each brake is connected to the hand lever by means of a flexible control cable. Usually, the LH lever controls the front brake, while the RH lever operates the rear brake, although they can be reversed according to your preference.

The now almost extinct, but by no means inferior, centerpull brakes, found on some older road bikes, have a connecting cable, also called straddle cable, between the two brake arms.

Brake Maintenance

From a maintenance standpoint, the brakes should be considered as

complete systems, each incorporating levers, control cables, and various pieces of mounting hardware, as well as the brake itself. In fact, brake problems are most often due to inadequacies of some component in the control system. Consequently, it will be necessary to approach the problem systematically, trying to isolate the fault by checking off one component after the other.

Left: applying the brake fully.
Right: typical modern sidepull brake.

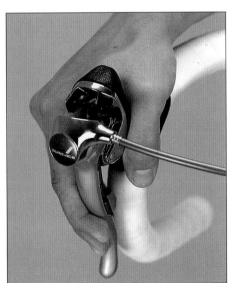

When the brakes work inconsistently, often with associated vibrations or squealing, the cause is usually found either in dirt and grease on the rims, loosely mounted fittings, or incorrect brake pad positioning. First check the condition of the rims, then the attachments of brake pads, brake arms, brake units, cables, anchors and levers. If the rim is dented, there is usually no other solution than to replace it, while all other causes can usually be eliminated quite easily.

Adjusting Brake Pads

This simple job is often not only the solution to squealing, rumbling, or vibrating noises, but may also solve inadequate braking performance and prevent serious mishaps. As the brake pad wears, its position relative to the rim changes.

Left: brake cable tension quick-release.
Right: This is how the brake pad is adjusted.

Check the position of the brake pads as they contact the rim, and readjust them if they don't align. It is preferable that the front end of the brake pad be about 1–2 mm closer to the rim than the rear. This is to compensate for the deformation of the brake arm as brake force is applied, which tends to twist the back of the brake pad in. Only when you adjust them this way, referred to as *toed in*, will the brake force be equally distributed over the entire length of the brake pad.

Tools and equipment:

pliers ; 5 mm Allen wrench; 9 mm wrench

Procedure:

1. Loosen the nut or bolt that holds the brake pad to the brake arm by about one turn.

2. While applying the corresponding brake lever with modest hand force, move the brake pads in the position illustrated, then increase lever force. You may have to twist the

brake pad and the underlying spherical and cupped washers—or whatever other device is provided for angular adjustment—to achieve this position.

3. Place a small piece of cardboard, about 1 mm ($\frac{1}{32}$–$\frac{1}{16}$ in.) thick between the brake pad and the rim, over the back 12 mm ($\frac{1}{2}$ in.) of the brake pad.

4. Holding the brake pad against the side of the rim firmly with the pliers, making sure it does not shift from its correct position, tighten the bolt fully.

5. Check to make sure the brake works correctly, and fine-tune the adjustment if necessary.

Brake Test

In order to verify their condition and effectiveness, test the brakes according to the following systematic procedure at regular intervals—about once a month under normal conditions. The idea is to establish whether the deceleration achieved with each brake is as high as the physical constraints of the bicycle's geometry will allow. Tools are not needed for this test.

Procedure:

1. Ride the bike at a brisk walking speed (about 8 km/h, or 5 m.p.h.) on a straight, level surface without traffic.

2. Apply the rear brake hard. If the rear wheel skids, you have all the

braking you can use in the rear—a deceleration of 3.5 m/sec^2.

3. Repeat the procedure with the front brake. But be careful—you don't want to go over the handlebars. If the rear wheel starts to lift off, a deceleration of 6.5 m/sec^2 has been reached, and that's as much as you'll ever want.

Brake System Inspection

If one brake or the other fails the test described above, or if you have other reasons to doubt your brake's performance, check the entire brake system and adjust or correct as necessary. Usually, no tools are needed for this inspection, but you may have to use a variety of items to solve individual problems uncovered this way.

Procedure:

1. Check to make sure the rim and the brake pads are clean. The presence of wet or greasy dirt plays havoc with their operation. Wipe clean or degrease the rim and scrape the brake pad with steel wire wool.

2. Check whether the cables move freely and are not pinched or damaged. Clean, free, and lubricate or replace cables that don't move freely. Repair or replace anything else found wanting.

3. Inspect the levers—they must be firmly installed and there must be at least 2 cm ($\frac{3}{4}$ in.) clearance between lever and handlebars

when the brake is applied fully. If necessary, tighten, lubricate, and adjust.

4. Make sure the brake arms themselves are free to move without resistance, and that they are returned to clear the wheel fully by the spring tension when the lever is released. If necessary, loosen, adjust, lubricate, overhaul, or replace.

Note on hydraulic brakes:

In the (rare) case of hydraulics, check for correct operation and installation. Except that there are no cables to get pinched, the rest is maintained the same way. And in addition, you may have a leaky seal, as evidenced by drops of liquids. If the system feels spongy, the reason may be air trapped inside. To eliminate it, follow the

Adjusting the brake by the barrel adjuster on the brake arm.

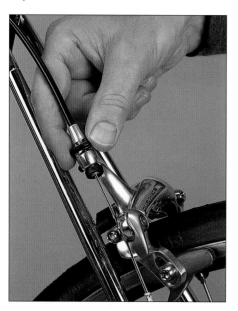

manufacturer's instruction on "bleeding" the system.

Adjusting Brakes

The most common type of brake adjustment is that required to tighten the cable a little in order to compensate for brake pad wear. First carry out the brake pad adjustment mentioned above, though. If you don't, there is a risk of the brake pad sooner or later slipping off the side of the rim and hitting the tire when you apply the brake.

Tools and equipment:

5 mm Allen wrench; 9 mm wrench; pliers

Procedure:

1. If the brake does not perform adequately, the cable tension must be increased. Do that initially by tightening the cable adjuster by two turns.

2. Verify whether the brake now engages fully when 2 cm (¾ in.) clearance remains between lever and handlebars.

3. If the correct adjustment cannot be achieved within the adjusting range of the cable adjuster, first screw it in all the way, then pull the cable further and tighten the clamping bolt again. On the centèrpull brake this can be done by wrapping the cable around the needle nose pliers and twisting it further. Now fine-tune with the adjuster.

4. If after all this adjusting the brake finally transmits enough tension but does not clear the rim adequately when disengaged, you will have to check all parts of the system and replace or overhaul as necessary.

Centering Brake

When the brake drags on one side or the other, the problem is due to the stubbornness of the mounting bolt, always twisting back into an off-center position. This is a problem almost inherent in sidepull brake design. Straightening is easier said than done: it will find its way back to this wrong position the next time the brake is applied.

Some brake models come with a special adjusting tool with which the mounting bolt is repositioned, each of them with its own instructions. There is also a universal tool, which may work on brakes without their own special tool: place each of the pins inside a loop of the spring and twist in the appropriate direction. On other models, for which no tool is provided, proceed as follows.

Tools and equipment:

13–14 mm cone wrench; 6 mm Allen wrench

Procedure:

1. If the mounting bolt has flats between the brake and the fork or the frame, place the cone wrench on these flats and the second wrench or Allen key on the nut at the end of the mounting bolt. If not, put a wrench on each end of the mounting bolt.

2. Older brakes may have two nuts on the top of the mounting bolt—the outside nut if you have to turn clockwise, the inside one to turn counterclockwise.

Left: centering a sidepull brake with built-in adjusting set screw.
Right: centering brake without, using a special tool to fit between the springs in the back.

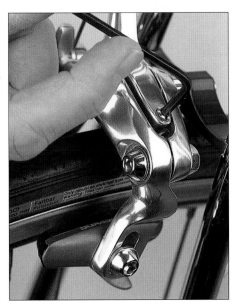

3. To twist the mounting bolt, turn both tools simultaneously.

If after all this the problem remains or returns, install a flat, thin steel washer between the brake body and the fork or rear stay bridge (or the shaped spacer installed there). This will provide a smooth "unbiased" surface that can be twisted into the desired position, rather than getting stuck in existing incorrect indentations.

Procedure for centerpull brakes:

On this type of brake found only on older road bikes, it is generally a simple matter of twisting the yoke on which the brake arms are installed in the right orientation.

1. First make sure the brake is firmly attached, tightening the mounting bolt if necessary, while depressing the lever and holding the brake centered.

2. If the brake is properly fastened and still off-set, you'll need a big screwdriver and a hammer. Place the screwdriver on the pivot point that is too high and lightly tap it with the hammer.

3. Repeat or correct until the brake is centered.

Overhauling or Replacing Brakes

Especially if the bike is frequently used in bad weather, this work is recommended once a year—or whenever the brake gives unsatisfactory performance and adjustment does not solve the problem. This work is most easily carried out while the wheel is removed.

If you are installing a new brake unit, rather than overhauling an old one, make sure the new unit has the right reach (the vertical distance between the mounting bolt and the position of the rim and the brake blocks) and opens up far enough to clear the rim on your bike. And of

Attachment of brake pad to brake arm.

The sidepull brake unit seen from the back, exposing the return spring.

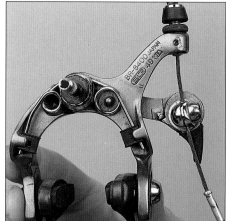

course, the brake lever has to be compatible with the brake unit itself.

Tools and equipment:

13–14 mm cone wrench; 5 mm Allen wrench; needle-nose pliers

Removal procedure:

1. Release the brake quick-release; then undo the cable at the brake.

2. Check the condition of the cable and replace it if necessary— remove the cable anchor clamp using a wrench on the nut and an Allen wrench on the bolt part. Pull the cable out, and later insert the new one. If an end cap is installed on the end of the cable, it must be pulled off with needle-nose pliers. I recommend soldering or crimping the end of the cable to prevent fraying, following the instructions under *Replacing Brake Cable.*

3. Unscrew the mounting bolt and remove the whole unit.

Installing the brake unit on the front fork.

4. Using the needle-nose pliers, remove the upper end of the spring of each brake arm from its seating, then pull the brake arm, the spring, and the bushing off the pivot stud.

5. Clean, inspect, and if necessary repair or replace any damaged parts. Most bike shops have a bin of discarded brake parts, from which you may be able to salvage replacements, otherwise they may have to be ordered; but given the price of a new brake unit, it's worthwhile trying to salvage what you can.

6. Remove the brake pads and their fixing bolts, in order to clean and if necessary to replace them (if the brake pads are badly worn).

Installation procedure:

1. After ascertaining that all parts are functional, clean, and, where appropriate, lightly greased, put the spring or springs back in place with the ends pushing the brake arms appart.

2. Reassemble the brake unit, making sure the brake arms are still free to move but not loose.

3. Put the washers or spacers that belong directly against the back of the brake in place on the mounting bolt.

4. Install the brake unit back on the fork or the frame bridge.

5. Attach the cable, then readjust the cable tension by adjusting at the cable adjuster or—if the deviation is significant—by clamping the

cable in at a different point on the cable.

6. Adjust the brake pad position as described under *Adjust Brake Pad*. Make sure the brake is installed centered, so both pads are equally far from the rim.

7. Carry out a brake test and make any final adjustments that may be necessary.

Brake Controls

The brakes are operated via handlebar-mounted levers, usually via flexible cables (a very rare exceptions is the hydraulically operated brake with oil-filled tubes instead of cables).

Left: modern integrated brake-and-gear lever, removed from handlebars and with brake cable exposed.
Right: loosening brake lever—this is a conventional non-integrated lever.

Adjusting Brake Lever

Although there are a number of different makes and models, even within the category of road bike brake levers, the similarities are generally so great that the following general description covers all but the most unusual models. All are designed to fit standard 22.2 mm (⅞ in.) diameter handlebars.

The levers are held to the handlebars by means of an internal clamp (referred to as pull strap) accessible after depressing the lever. The cable on modern levers for drop handlebars no longer comes out of the top but at the bottom near the clamp and is routed along the handlebars.

The brake lever must be installed so that it can be easily reached and pulled in so far that the brake is fully applied when a gap of about 20 mm (¾ in.) remains between the brake lever and the handlebars at the tightest point. There are four forms of

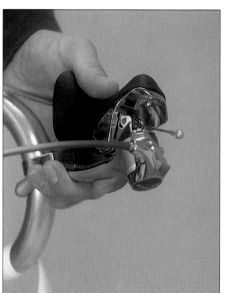

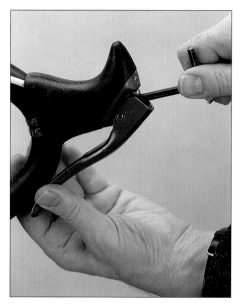

adjustment that apply to the brake lever:

- ☐ mounting position
- ☐ reach
- ☐ cable routing
- ☐ cable tension

Tools and equipment:

5 mm Allen wrench; 9–10 mm wrench; small screwdriver (for older models)

Procedure—position adjustment:

1. Determine in which direction the brake lever should be moved or rotated to provide adequate and comfortable operation.

2. Establish whether the handlebar tape or any other items installed on the handlebars may have to be removed in order to allow for the relocation of the brake lever to the desired position. Loosen these parts, so they can be easily moved.

3. Using the wrench, loosen the clamp that holds the lever to the handlebars by one or two turns, then twist or slide the lever to its desired location and tighten the clamping bolt again. Make sure the lever does not extend beyond the end of the handlebars. You want to avoid accidental brake application while passing closely by any objects in your path behind which the brake levers might get caught.

4. Most road bikes have an internal bolt that can be reached once the lever is pulled, best done after removing the cable. On old models it requires a screwdriver, while more recent versions

require the use of a 5 mm Allen key. Make sure not to unscrew this bolt all the way, because it will be hard to reinstall.

5. Retighten any other components that may have been moved to new locations; make sure all parts are really in their most convenient position and are properly tightened.

Procedure—reach adjustment:

1. Unlike mountain bike brake levers, there is no adjusting screw for reach adjustment on road bike brake levers. All you can do is mount the lever in a different location along the bend.

2. Check the distance between the handlebars and the brake lever in the unapplied position compared with the maximum comfortable

The brake hood pulled away to reveal the attachment.

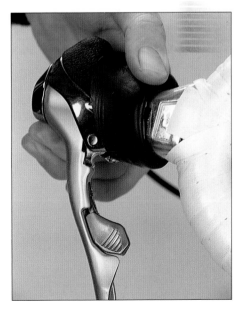

reach of your hand. In general, it should be opened as far as possible commensurate with the size of your hand, since a larger reach allows the most effective brake application and the most accurate adjustment of the brake cable.

3. If adjustment is necessary, loosen the mounting bolt per the preceding description, then move the unit up or down until you have achieved the optimal position commensurate with the distance in depressed and released positions.

4. Check to make sure the brake can be applied properly, and adjust the brake cable, following the appropriate instructions below, if necessary.

5. Tighten the lever down firmly.

Conventional (non-integrated) brake lever being removed from the handlebars.

Replacing or Overhauling Brake Lever

Before removing or installing a brake lever, remove the handlebar tape from the handlebars. Loosen the brake cable (as described above) if the lever is to be replaced by another one. Usually a stiff operating lever can be freed by replacing the bushings or by bending the metal around the pivot out a little. If not, you may have to replace the entire lever.

Tools and equipment:

screwdriver or Allen wrench (depending on the type of internal attachment bolt, reached when the lever is pulled)

Removal procedure:

1. Release tension on the brake cable (either with the quick-release or with the cable-attachment bolt).

2. Depress the lever; push the cable inside the lever to one side to gain access to the internal bolt. Loosen the bolt about three full turns—not so far that it comes out of its special nut, since it is hard to get it back in before installing the lever. The strap with which the lever is clamped around the handlebars opens up a little this way.

3. Push the lever assembly off the handlebar ends, in a twisting movement if it becomes tight, loosening the bolt further if it will not come off any other way.

Installation procedure:

1. Make sure the lever used is correct for the handlebars and the brake installed on the bike. Replace the cable if it is not in perfect condition.

2. Unscrew the internal bolt in the lever just far enough to loosen the attachment strap—not so far that it will come out of the special nut—if it does, it will be tricky to put it back in.

3. Slide the lever over the end of the handlebars into the correct position. Check the position to make sure it can be reached and fully contracted easily with the whole hand—moving it farther up or down the bend in the handlebars or angling it in or out will often improve these things. If the strap will not fit around the bars, it is the wrong size.

4. Tighten the bolt when the bars are in the right position; then install the cable as described above, making any adjustments to the brake that may be called for.

Adjusting Brake Cable

The main brake adjustment—the only one usually required from time to time to compensate for brake pad wear—is that of the brake cable. To adjust the brake cable tension, either the lever or the brake unit is equipped with a barrel adjuster. In case the adjusting range of this device is not adequate, the attachment of the cable to the brake itself can be changed. The latter adjustment depends on the type of brake used, but the instructions can be generalized enough to cover most situations.

Tools and equipment:

needle-nose pliers; 5 mm Allen wrench or 9 mm wrench

Procedure:

1. If the brake does not apply adequate force when the lever is pulled, the cable must be tightened. If, on the other hand, the brake seems to be applied too soon—if the brake scrapes the side of the rim when the lever is not pulled—it should be slackened a little.

2. To tighten the brake cable, hold the locknut and screw the barrel

On the lever side, this is the way the cable comes out and is then taped along the handlebars.

adjuster out by several turns. Then hold the barrel adjuster in place, while screwing in the locknut.

3. To release the brake cable, hold the barrel adjuster and back off the locknut by several turns, then screw the barrel adjuster in further, and finally tighten the locknut, while holding the barrel adjuster to stop it from turning.

4. Check and readjust, if necessary, until operation of the brake is optimal.

5. If the adjusting range of the barrel adjuster is not adequate, screw it in all the way, after having backed off the locknut fully. Then proceed to adjust the clamping position of the cable at the brake.

Flip the brake quick-release. And don't forget to tension it again afterwards.

6. The end of the cable at the brake unit itself is clamped onto an anchor by means of either an eye bolt or a pinch plate held under a bolt-and-nut combination. Loosen the nut of this unit and pull the cable through a little further, then clamp it in properly at the new position by tightening the nut while holding the bolt.

7. Check once more and adjust the barrel adjuster at the brake lever if necessary.

Replacing Brake Cable

This should be done about once a year—or whenever the cable is pinched, corroded or otherwise damaged, especially if signs of broken strands are in evidence. Make sure you get a model that has the same kind of nipple (visible inside the lever) as the old one.

Tools and equipment:

5 mm Allen wrench or 9 mm wrench; cable cutters; grease; soldering equipment or crimping tool

Removal procedure:

1. Release tension on the brake by squeezing the brake arms against the rim, then release the cable.

2. Unscrew the eye bolt or clamp nut that holds the cable to the brake arm (or, on a centerpull brake, to the triangular plate over which the straddle cable runs), making sure not to lose the various parts.

3. Push the cable through towards the lever, then pull it out once enough slack is generated, catching any pieces of outer cable and end pieces.

4. Remove the cable, dislodging the nipple from the lever.

Installation procedure:

1. Establish whether the outer cable is still intact and replace it if necessary, cutting it to length in such a way that no hook is formed at the end (bending the metal of the spiral back if necessary).

2. Lubricate the inner cable with grease.

3. Place the nipple in the lever and guide the cable through the lever and the cable casing (and, in the case of a centerpull brake, the various stops and guides).

Left: pulling the cable tight at the brake unit.
Right: cutting off the end of the cable. If you con't solder the end of the inner cable, at least crimp on an end cap to prevent fraying.

4. Attach the end in the eye bolt or clamp nut at the brake.

5. Adjust the cable tension as described above.

6. If you have the equipment to do it, solder the strands of the inner cable together at the end to prevent fraying, before you cut it off.

7. Cut off the excess cable length, leaving about 2.5–3 cm (1–1¼ in.) projecting. This is best done with special cable cutters, although it can be done with other sharp and strong pliers, such as diagonal cutters.

8. If you cannot solder the end of the cable, crimp on an end cap.

Brake Squeal and Jitter

These two disturbing phenomena of rim brake operation are at opposite ends of the danger scale: squeal is

Tightening the brake pad attachment.

quite harmless, and really little more than an embarrassment; brake jitter can disturb steering and balancing enough to cause a danger to the rider.

A squealing brake may be silenced by cleaning the rim, by choosing a different brake pad material, by using non-anodized aluminum rims, or by fine-tuning the toeing-in of the brake pads somewhat. The latter operation brings the front end of the brake pads a little closer to the rim than the back—the braking force will then straighten out the pad again once the brake is applied. If the brake is not

adjustable in this direction (some brakes have spherical inserts to do just that), you will have to bend the brake arm into the desired shape using two crescent wrenches—if you have the nerve for it. In some persistent cases, I've found that actually toeing the pads *out*, instead of *in*, solved the problem—experiment a little before you give up.

Brake jitter is either caused by looseness in the brake mounting bolt or the pivots, by unevenness in the side of the rim, or by excessive flexibility in the fork, and may be aggravated by loose head-set bearings. So those are the things to check and to correct, although at least one of these factors—flexibility in the fork—cannot be eliminated, except by replacing the entire fork. In my experience, fork flexibility should only be seen as an aggravating factor, increasing the effect of other factors. When the other problem is corrected, the brake will not jitter, even with a flexible fork. It is likely that choosing different brake pad materials may also alleviate the problem to some extent—experiment around, once you have eliminated the most dangerous causes and the symptoms have not complete disappeared.

Chapter 11

The Steering System

The steering system is crucial for control over the bike, even when going straight. The parts of the steering system are shown below: front fork, headset bearings, stem, and handlebars.

The handlebars are connected to the front fork's steerer tube by means of a stem. The bars are clamped in the stem's collar with a binder bolt. Virtually all road bikes use a headset screwed onto the fork's steerer tube. Lately, though, a few road bikes have come out with a threadless headset borrowed from mountain bike technology.

On bikes with a conventional headset that use a threaded steerer tube, the stem is clamped inside by means of a wedge-shaped (or more rarely a cone-shaped) device. This is pulled into the bottom of the stem with the expander bolt, accessible from the top of the stem and usually equipped with a 6 mm hexagonal recess for an Allen key. Allen bolts are also used to clamp the handlebars in the stem.

On those rare bikes with a threadless headset, the stem is clamped around the headset, and the bolt on top of the stem is used only to adjust the headset bearing (but only while the stem clamp is loosened).

Left: tightening or loosening the expander bolt that holds the handlebar stem in the bike's steerer tube.
Right: tightening or loosening the Allen bolt that clamps the handlebars in the stem.

Handlebars and Stem

The handlebar jobs most typically required are to adjust the height, to straighten the bars, or to replace either part. Most road bike handlebars are ⅞ in. (22.2 mm) diameter, with a 26 or 27 mm bulge where it is clamped into the stem. Make sure stem and handlebars match when replacing either one. If the handlebars are too close to, or too far from, the rider, the stem must be replaced by a longer or shorter model.

Adjusting or Tightening Handlebars

This is required when the bike is set up for a different rider, when the position proves uncomfortable, or when the handlebars are not firmly in place. The description is based on a conventional headset.

Tools and equipment:

Allen key; sometimes a mallet or a hammer

Procedure:

1. If appropriate (i.e. to adjust), loosen the attachment of the stem by unscrewing the expander bolt 2–3 turns.

2. Straddle the front wheel, keeping it straight relative to the bike's frame, and put the handlebars in the required position as regards height and orientation, holding them steady with one hand.

3. If the stem won't turn or move, unscrew the expander bolt another 4–6 turns, lift the wheel

off the ground, supporting the bike from the handlebars, then tap on the expander bolt with the mallet, after which it will usually come loose. If it doesn't, apply some spray lubricant between the stem and the collar or locknut at the top of the headset and try again.

4. Still holding firmly, tighten the expander bolt.

5. Verify whether the handlebars are now in the right position and make any corrections that may be necessary.

Threadless headset note:

The handlebar height on a bike with these newfangled headsets can only be varied by means of a different stem, one with more or less rise.

Tightening Handlebars in Stem

The connection between the handlebars and the stem should also be firm, so the handlebars don't twist out of their proper orientation. Do this by simply tightening the bolts that clamp the stem collar around the bars, using a matching Allen key.

Replacing Handlebars with Stem

This has to be done when the bars are bent or otherwise damaged, when you want to install a different design, or in the context of a general overhauling operation of the bike.

Tools and equipment:

Allen wrench; cloth; lubricant

Removal procedure:

1. Loosen all cables leading to items installed on the handlebars (gear and brake levers).

2. Using the Allen wrench, loosen the expander bolt by 3–4 turns, or until the stem is obviously loose.

3. If the stem doesn't come loose, unscrew the expander bolt 4–6 more turns, lift the wheel off the ground, holding the bike by the handlebars, then tap on the expander bolt with the mallet, after which it will usually come loose. If it doesn't, apply some spray lubricant between the stem and the collar or locknut at the top of the headset and try again.

4. Remove the handlebars complete with the stem.

Installation procedure:

1. Clean the stem and the inside of the fork's steerer tube with a clean rag, then put some grease on the wedge (or the cone) and the part of the stem that will go inside the steerer tube, in order to prevent rust and to ease subsequent adjustment or replacement.

2. Tighten the expander bolt so far that the wedge is snug up to the stem's slanted end in the right orientation, still allowing free movement of the stem in the steerer tube.

3. If a cone-shape device is used instead of a wedge, align the ribs

on the cone with the slots in the end of the stem.

4. Install the stem and position it in the correct orientation.

5. Straddle the front wheel, keeping it straight relative to the bike's frame, and put the handlebars in the required position as regards height and orientation, holding them steady with one hand.

6. Still holding the handlebars firmly in place, tighten the expander bolt.

7. Verify whether the handlebars are now in the right position and make any necessary corrections.

The handlebar-and-stem combination removed from the bike.

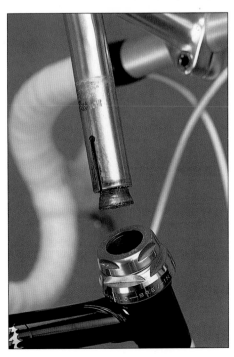

Threadless headset note:

On bikes with threadless headsets (still rare on road bikes), the stem is not wedged inside the fork's steerer tube but clamped around it by means of two clamp bolts. The dustcap at the top of the stem hides a bolt, but this one is used only to adjust the headset bearing, not to remove the stem.

Replacing Handlebars or Stem

This must be done when the handlebars are seriously damaged or when you want to install another model. First check whether the new handlebars have the same diameter as the old ones—if not, also replace the stem.

Tools and equipment:

Allen wrench; large screwdriver; tools to replace items installed on the handlebars

Removal procedure:

1. Remove the handlebar tape and any components installed on the handlebars.

2. Loosen and remove the binder bolts clamping the stem collar around the handlebars.

3. Using the big screwdriver, spread open the collar and pull the thicker section of the handlebars out of the collar; then release the screwdriver, and twist the handlebars in such a way as to find the most favorable orientation along its bend while pulling it out.

Installation procedure:

1. Push the handlebars through the collar, twisting to ease it around the curve, until the thicker section is reached, then open up the collar with the big screwdriver.

2. Bring the handlebars to the correct location.

3. Install the bolts and partially tighten them.

4. Adjust the bars in the exact location desired and hold them there firmly while tightening the bolts.

5. Install all the components required on the handlebars, following the appropriate instructions in the relevant chapters.

6. Check the position and orientation again, making any adjustments that may be necessary.

7. Reinstall the handlebar tape.

Triathlon Bars and Extensions

These devices are used to allow the more forward-leaning aerodynamic position associated with triathlon and other forms of time trialing, where steering control of the bike is less critical than any aerodynamic advantage. They're differently shaped, but installed the same way as regular handlebars.

In many cases, clip-on extensions are used that are mounted on regular drop bars. When installing or adjusting these, make sure they are bolted down so tightly that they can not slip.

Replacing Handlebar Tape

Drop handlebars are usually covered with handlebar tape, which has to be replaced when it gets uncomfortable or unsightly owing to wear or damage. You will also have to rewrap it if it has been removed in order to replace a brake lever or the stem. Since brake cables are generally routed along the bars, you will have to rewrap when replacing an outer cable. Choose either non-adhesive cork, plastic, or cloth tape, or tape with a narrow adhesive backing strip. At least one roll of tape is needed for each side. Nowadays, most sets of handlebar tape come with two short pre-cut pieces to be used at the brake hoods where the handlebars are bare.

Procedure:

1. Remove the old handlebar tape after loosening the handlebar end plugs. Adhesive tape may have to be cut, after which it is advisable to clean the adhesive off with methylated spirit. Lift the rubber brake hoods off the levers so they clear the handlebars and place the short sections of tape there.

2. Adhesive tape is wound starting from a point about 7.5 cm (3 in.) from the center, working towards the ends. Overlap each layer generously with the preceding one and wrap in an X-pattern around the brake lever attachments.

3. Non-adhesive tape is wound starting from the ends, after tucking a piece inside. Work towards the center, and overlap as described above for adhesive

Left: handlebar taping detail at the brake-lever attachment.
Right: installing end cap on handlebar ends.

tape. Fasten the ends by wrapping some adhesive tape around them.

4. Install the end plugs, and tighten them with a screwdriver if they have an expander screw in the end.

The Headset

The headset is the double set of ball bearings with which the steering system is pivoted in the frame. By way of regular maintenance, it should occasionally be lubricated and perhaps overhauled, or—when it can't be adjusted to satisfaction—it may have to be replaced.

Although the conventional type is still very much more common on road bikes than it is on mountain bikes, headsets come in two distinct types: the conventional ones threaded onto the fork's steerer tube, and the threadless headset type, which fits on a smooth steerer tube (and thus requires a corresponding unthreaded fork). The latter type is adjusted via a bolt that is reached from the top of the stem.

Adjusting Conventional Headset

Once a season—and whenever the steering is rough or loose—adjust the bearings as follows:

Tools and equipment:

headset wrenches or large crescent wrenches

Procedure:

1. Loosen the collar or locknut on the upper headset by about one turn (after loosening a set screw on some models).

2. Lift the washer under this nut enough to release the underlying part, which is the adjustable bearing cup.

3. Tighten or loosen the adjustable bearing cup by turning it to the right or the left, respectively.

4. Put the washer in place and tighten the collar or locknut, holding the adjustable cup in place.

5. Check to make sure the adjustment is correct—not too loose and not too tight. Readjust if necessary, following the same procedure.

Note:

If adjusting does not solve your problem, the headset must be overhauled according to the following description.

Overhauling Conventional Headset

The same disassembly and installation procedures are followed when either the headset or the fork is to be replaced.

Tools and equipment:

headset wrenches or large crescent wrenches; tools to remove handlebars and brake; bearing grease; cloths

Disassembly procedure:

1. Remove the handlebars with the stem as described above and loosen the front brake cable; then remove the front wheel, after unhooking or relaxing tension on the front brake cable.

2. Loosen and remove the collar or locknut on top of the headset.

3. Remove the lockwasher by lifting it straight off.

4. Unscrew the adjustable bearing cup, while holding the fork to the frame.

5. Remove the bearing balls, which are usually held in a bearing ball retainer.

6. Pull the fork out from the frame, also catching the lower bearing balls, again usually held in a retainer.

Inspection and overhauling procedure:

1. Inspect all parts for wear, corrosion, and damage, evidenced by pitting or grooves.

2. Replace the entire headset if significant damage is apparent; always use new bearing balls, either loose or in a retainer to match the particular size of headset installed.

3. If the headset has to be replaced, it is preferable to have the fixed cups and the fork race removed (and new ones installed) with special tools at the bike shop.

4. Should you have the desire to do part of this job yourself using improvised tools, use a big

screwdriver and a hammer to remove the cups, and prize off the fork crown with a big screwdriver. But get the new ones installed with special tools at the bike shop.

Installation procedure:

1. If the fixed cups and the fork race are intact—or once they have been replaced—fill the bearing cups with bearing grease.

2. Hold the frame upside down and embed one of the bearing retainers in the grease-filled lower fixed bearing race (which is now facing up). The retainer must be installed in such a way that the bearing balls—not the metal ring—contact the inside of the cup.

Tightening or loosening the headset, shown here with the handlebars and the stem removed.

3. Hold the fork upside-down and put it through the head tube.

4. Turn the frame the right way round again, while holding the fork in place.

5. Embed the other bearing retainer in the grease-filled upper fixed bearing cup.

6. Screw the adjustable bearing cup onto the threaded end of the fork's steerer tube by hand.

7. Place the lock washer on top of the adjustable cup, and do the same with any part that may be installed to serve as a brake cable anchor or a spacer.

8. Screw the collar or locknut onto the threaded end of the steerer tube, without tightening it completely.

9. Install the front wheel.

The parts of a threadless headset.

10. Adjust the bearing as outlined above.

11. Check and, if necessary, correct any adjustments of the handlebars and the front brake.

Maintenance of Threadless Headset

These special headsets are adjusted by means of an Allen bolt on top of the special stem used with these headsets, after loosening the stem clamp and any other clamped parts. To tighten the headset, turn the bolt to the right; to loosen it, turn the bolt to the left—about 1/8 of a turn at a time until it feels right. Overhauling is actually easier than it is for a regular headset.

Tools and equipment:

Allen wrenches; rags; grease

Disassembly and overhauling procedure:

1. Remove the bolt and the cap from the top of the stem.

2. Remove the stem by undoing the Allen bolts that clamp it around the top of the fork's steerer tube.

3. Remove any spacers and brake cable hanger that may be installed between the stem and the upper headset bearing.

4. Hold the fork to the frame, and pull the conical compression ring off toward the top of the steerer tube, followed by the upper headset bearing.

5. Pull the fork out from the frame and remove the lower headset bearing.

6. Clean, lubricate, and overhaul the bearings just as you would a regular headset.

Installation Procedure:

1. Follow steps 1–5 of the general procedures for bearing installation under *Overhauling Conventional Headset* above.

2. Hold the fork in place and install the upper bearing race, then the conical compression ring with the skinny end first.

3. Install the stem around the top end of the steerer tube, but do not tighten the stem-clamping bolts yet.

4. Install the cap and the Allen bolt in the top of the stem so the bolt's threading engages the thread in the threaded insert inside the steerer tube, and *gently* tighten the bolt until the bearing feels right.

5. Hold the handlebars straight and tighten the stem's binder bolts.

Note:

The special fork with an unthreaded steerer tube used with the Aheadset is equipped with a star-shaped threaded insert. It may have to be replaced if you accidentally force it out. Install it from the top, using a piece of pipe or conduit that just fits inside the steerer tube.

The Front Fork

Most road bikes have a fork consisting of separate blades and a crown with which they are attached to the steerer tube, as opposed to the unicrown (inverted U) forks often used on mountain bikes. But there are differences between them, primarily on account of the headset bearing used—threaded or unthreaded (the latter for use with the Aheadset). Although the threading standard in use today is common, older bikes may have French threading, which has a slightly different size—don't force things.

If the steering gets sticky when turning the bars, even though it seems fine when going straight, it is due to a bent head tube, usually as a result of a collision. When replacing a fork that is bent, make sure the bosses installed for the brakes are in the right

Replacing the fork is an opportunity to overhaul the headset: keep it greased.

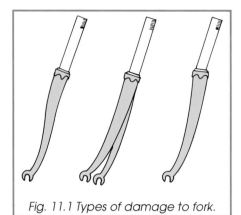

Fig. 11.1 Types of damage to fork.

shop, since the screw thread often has to be recut too. If you do decide to do it yourself, first screw the locknut on as a guide so you'll cut straight. File any burrs off the end before installing the fork.

Tools and equipment:

headset wrenches or large crescent wrenches; tools to remove handlebars and front brake

location for the kind of brakes used, and check the length of the steerer tube, which must also be the same as the old one—assuming it was correct. To determine the required steerer tube length, deduct 2 mm (3⁄32 in.) from the sum of the stacking height of the headset (given by the manufacturer) and the length of the head tube.

Front Fork Inspection

This is necessary whenever you have had a serious crash or when the bike does not seem to steer the way it should. Generally, a visual check is adequate, referring to Fig. 11.1 for the typical kinds of damage possible.

Replacing Front Fork

Although it may sometimes be possible to straighten a bent fork, I suggest you replace the entire fork, giving yourself a margin of safety that may prevent a bad crash later on. Sometimes the fork's steerer tube has to be cut shorter to fit the frame. It is preferable to have that done at a bike

Procedure:

1. Untension the cable for the front brake and remove the entire front brake; then remove the front wheel following the appropriate procedure in Chapter 5.

2. Remove the handlebars with the stem, following the description elsewhere in this chapter.

3. Disassemble the upper headset as outlined in the relevant description above.

4. Remove the fork, following the same description.

5. If necessary, use the fork as a reference to buy the new one, taking it to the bike shop with you.

6. Install the fork and the headset as described for the installation of the headset.

7. Install the handlebars as described above.

8. Install the front brake and hook up the cable.

9. Check and, if necessary, adjust all parts affected: headset, handlebars, front brake.

Chapter 12

Saddle and Seatpost

Although the saddle and seatpost are not among the most trouble-prone components on the bike, they do justify some attention. Here I will describe how to adjust the position of the saddle (also called seat), how to replace the saddle and the seatpost, and how to carry out any maintenance needed on a leather saddle.

On the road bike, the binder, or clamp, bolt generally is an Allen bolt, rather than the quick-release mechanism used on mountain bikes. The most common jobs on the saddle include height and position adjustment, and replacement of one part or another.

Adjusting Saddle Height

The saddle position should be adjusted whenever the bike is set up

for another rider or when the position is uncomfortably high or low for the present rider. Any regular bike book explains in detail how the correct height is determined—here you'll just be shown how to make the adjustment.

Tools and equipment:

Allen wrench, sometimes two (on older bikes a 12 or 13 mm open-ended or box wrench)

Procedure:

1. Loosen the Allen bolt on the RH side in order to loosen the

Left: saddle and seatpost.
Right: adjusting detail.

seatpost. On older bikes, unscrew the nut.

2. The seatpost with the saddle should now be free to move up and down. If it is not, apply some penetrating lubricant between the seatpost and the seat lug, wait a minute or two, and try again, if necessary twisting the saddle with the seatpost relative to the frame.

3. Place the saddle in the desired position. If penetrating oil was needed, first remove the seatpost all the way, then clean the seatpost and the interior of the seat tube and apply some grease to the outside of the seatpost before inserting it again.

4. Holding the saddle at the correct height and aligned perfectly straight forward, tighten the Allen bolt (or the nut).

5. Check whether the saddle is now installed firmly. If not, loosen the binder bolt, readjust, and try again.

Seat angle adjustment.

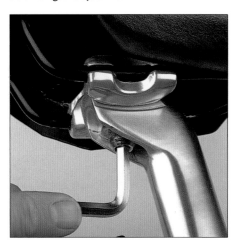

Adjusting Saddle Angle and Position

Generally, both of these adjustments are carried out with the same bolts that hold the saddle to the seatpost, which can be reached from under the saddle (except on some older special models).

Tools and equipment:

Allen key or other wrench to fit seatpost adjusting bolts

Procedure:

1. If the saddle must be moved forward or backward, loosen both bolts by about one or two turns each.

2. Holding the clamp on top of the seatpost with one hand and the saddle with the other, move the saddle into the correct position.

3. If the saddle merely has to be tipped, i.e., the front raised or lowered relative to the rear portion, loosen the nuts, and then move the saddle into the desired orientation.

4. Holding the saddle in the correct position, tighten the bolts, while preventing the saddle from moving.

5. Check and readjust if necessary.

Replacing Saddle with Seatpost

It is usually easier to remove the combination of saddle and seatpost than to remove the saddle alone. This is also the first step in removing the seatpost.

Tools and equipment:

cloth; grease or wax; Allen wrench (or regular wrench)

Removal procedure:

1. Unscrew the binder bolt until the seatpost can be moved up or down freely, as described under *Adjusting Saddle Height.*

2. Pull the saddle with the seatpost out of the frame's seat tube.

Installation procedure:

1. Clean the outside of the seatpost and the inside of the seat tube, then smear grease, wax, or vaseline on the seatpost to prevent corrosion and to ease subsequent adjustments.

2. Install the seatpost with the saddle, and adjust it to the correct height.

3. Tighten the binder bolt as described under *Adjusting Saddle Height.*

Note:

If adjustment problems persist, especially if the seatpost won't come loose, it may be necessary to drill out the hole at the bottom of the slot in the rear of the seat lug to about 3 mm (⅛ in.)—or drill such a hole there if there is not one, since it prevents the formation of cracks and eases clamping or unclamping the lug around the seatpost.

Replacing Seatpost or Saddle

Not exactly a job that is often necessary, except if a new saddle or seatpost has to be installed—or to get water out of the frame. Just the same, here's how to go about it.

Left: attachment of saddle to seatpost. Right: details of seatpost clamp that holds the saddle.

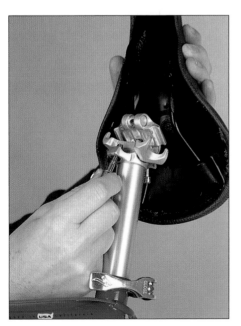

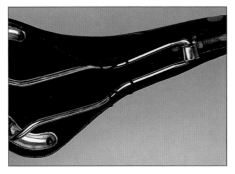

Leather saddle details.
Left: salvaging spread cover.
Right: tensioning cover.

Tools and equipment:

Allen wrench or other wrench to fit bolts that hold saddle to seatpost; sometimes wrench

Removal procedure:

1. For the time being, leave the saddle installed on the seatpost and remove the seatpost complete with the saddle as described under *Replacing Saddle with Seatpost.*

2. Separate the saddle from the seatpost by unscrewing the bolts that hold the saddle's wires to the seatpost clamp.

Installation procedure:

1. Install the saddle on the seatpost.

2. Install the seatpost with the saddle as described under *Replacing Saddle with Seatpost.*

3. Adjust the height, the forward position, and the angle of the saddle as described in the relevant sections above.

4. Check and readjust if necessary.

Maintenance of Leather Saddle

If you use a real leather saddle (as opposed to the usual nylon one with a thin leather cover), make sure it does not get wet. Wrap a plastic bag around the saddle when transporting the bike or leaving it outside when there is the slightest chance of rain. If it does get wet, don't sit on it until it is thoroughly dried out, since otherwise it will deform permanently. To keep it water resistant and slightly flexible, treat it with leather treatment such as Brooks Proofide at least twice a year.

Adjust the tension of a leather saddle no more than once a year and only when it has sagged noticeably, tightening the bolt shown in the illustration perhaps one turn at the most. Don't overdo this adjustment, since it often causes the saddle to be pulled into an uncomfortable shape.

Chapter 13

The Frame

Although the frame is the bicycle's biggest single part, it is fortunately rarely in need of maintenance or repair work. And when something does happen, it is likely to be so serious that the average rider decides to call it a day and perhaps even abandon the bike. Just the same, there are some maintenance aspects of the frame, which will be covered here.

Frame Construction

The photo below shows how the frame of your road bike is usually constructed (if you have a carbon-fiber frame, it may be made out of one piece instead of a bundle of tubes as shown). The front part, or main frame, is made up of large-diameter tubes, called the top tube, downtube, seat tube and head tube. The bottom bracket shell is located at its lowest point. The rear triangle is built up of double sets of smaller-diameter tubes, called seat stays and chain stays. Each pair is connected by means of a short bridge piece.

Most road bike frames are constructed by brazing (using silver- or bronze-solder) the tubes together by means of lugs as shown. Some frames are built with fillet-brazed joints, where the tubes are brazed directly together with smooth contours. Some frames are built the way most mountain bikes are built, namely TIG-welded—the joints will look a little more abrupt but the quality can be just as good as using the other methods. Some frames may have bonded joints, or the entire frame is built up in one piece of resin-bonded carbon-fiber or Kevlar composite.

General view of the bare frame for a road bike.

Whether welded, brazed, or bonded, one lug is always present: the seat lug. It is split in the back and clamped together to hold the saddle. At the ends where the stays meet there are flat plates, called drop-outs, into which the wheels are installed. The one on the right also contains a threaded eye, in which the derailleur is mounted. Finally, there are a number of small parts, referred to as braze-ons. These include shifter bosses, bosses for the installation of water bottles, and cable stops and guides.

Although most frames are made of some kind of steel tubing, quite a few bike frames are made of aluminum (these are generally the frames with large diameter tubes) or titanium (the most expensive ones). Neither material is inherently superior to the other. In fact, aluminum and titanium frames are

Detail of bottom bracket area.

not necessarily lighter than steel frames in the corresponding price range, due to the larger tube diameters required for adequate strength and rigidity. Titanium is always welded; most aluminum frames are welded, while some are bonded together with the aid of internal or external lugs. Finally, there are composite frames made in part with resin-embedded carbon or Kevlar fibers.

Frame Damage

Bike frames sometimes get damaged in transportation or in a fall or accident. In case of a head-on collision, the first thing to bend is the front fork (discussed in Chapter 11), but there is a chance of the downtube literally buckling at a point just behind the head tube. Left unchecked, this will eventually lead to the frame's collapse, which can be highly dangerous. It's the kind of damage only a professional frame builder can solve for you and one that's only worthwhile on an expensive frame: the downtube has to be removed and replaced by a new one. After a serious head-on collision, check the appropriate location for damage. If it is buckled, take the bike to a bike shop to find out what can be done about it.

Other kinds of frame damage are less dramatic, though they may be serious enough. A collision, a fall or other forms of abuse may cause the frame to go out of alignment. You can verify this from time to time by trying to line up front and rear wheel while looking from behind. If it can't be done, either the frame or the front fork is probably misaligned. The descriptions below show you how to check the frame and what to do about it. Finally, it sometimes happens that one of the drop-outs gets bent—usually the one with the RH derailleur eye, which results in poor gear shifting. Instructions to establish and correct this problem are also included below.

Frame Alignment Check

In this and the following procedures, all the checks that can be carried out relatively simply will be described in some detail. Always see a bike shop about correcting any damage detected.

Tools and equipment:

3 m (10 ft.) of twine; ruler marked in mm or 32nds

Procedure:

1. Remove the rear wheel from the bike, following the relevant description in Chapter 5.

2. Wrap the twine around the frame, pulling it taut at the drop-outs.

3. Measure and compare the distance between seat tube and twine on both sides. If the difference is more than 3 mm (⅛ in.), the frame is out of alignment and should be corrected.

Rear-Triangle Alignment

Occasionally, the misalignment is due to a minor deformation of the tubes of the rear triangle. If this is the case, you may be able to correct it yourself—at least on most steel frames (it can't be done on composite frames, and is not safe to do on aluminum, titanium, and very light steel frames). Check the tubes of the rear triangle for serious and abrupt

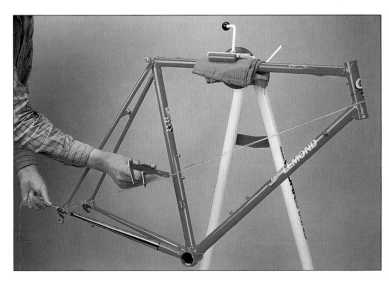

Checking a frame for alignment.

damage. If this is the case, get advice from a bike mechanic. If not, proceed with the correction procedure described here, repeating the preceding check as you continue, to verify you don't make the situation worse.

Tools and equipment:

none required, but two people are needed to carry out the work

Procedure:

1. Place the frame on a solid raised surface, such as a work bench, with the side of the rear triangle that has to be bent out (as established in the preceding check) facing down, or the part that has to be bent in facing up.

2. One person stands on the main frame at seat tube and head tube.

Drop-out detail.

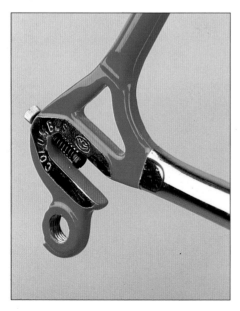

3. The other person carefully forces the rear triangle in the required direction.

4. Check frame alignment and repeat the operation until you are satisfied.

Note:

Although this kind of work can be done quite satisfactorily on a steel frame if you are careful, it is generally preferable to consult an experienced bike mechanic and have him or her do the work for you. This applies especially on light frames; Kevlar and carbon-fiber frames just can't be corrected for love or money.

Checking Drop-Outs

After a fall, the reason for derailleur problems may be that the rear derailleur eye (on the RH rear drop-out) is bent. In other cases, the wheel just doesn't want to center, even though it seems to be undamaged (as checked in Chapter 5). To establish whether the drop-outs are still straight after a fall or rough transportation—this damage is more typically caused by the latter—proceed as follows:

Tools and equipment:

60 cm (2 ft.) long metal straightedge

Procedure:

1. Remove the rear wheel from the bike, following the relevant procedure in Chapter 5.

2. Hold the straightedge snug up against the outside of the RH

drop-out, holding, but not forcing, the other end near the downtube, and measure the distance between the straight-edge and the seat tube.

3. Repeat step 2 for the LH drop-out.

4. Compare the distance of the straightedge from the seat tube on both sides, referring to the dimension lines shown in the illustration.

5. Measure the distance between the drop-outs and compare it with the sum of the seat tube diameter and the two distances just measured.

6. If the difference is more than 3 mm (⅛ in.), at least one of the drop-outs should be straightened—preferably by the bike mechanic, but you may want to try your hand at it yourself. Usually, you can tell by means of a visual inspection which is the one that's bent.

Aligning Drop-outs

After the preceding check, you may want to straighten a bent drop-out. However, don't do it if cracks are visible at any point or if the derailleur mounting lug (with its threaded hole) is bent relative to the rest of the drop-out. Leave such problems to a bike mechanic, who has a special tool for this job. The same goes for composite and aluminum frames—the aluminum drop-outs used on those tend to crack, if not when they get bent in the first place, then when you try to straighten them.

Tools and equipment:

vise with soft metal protectors, mounted on a work bench

Procedure:

1. Establish whether it is just the derailleur eye or the drop-out itself that is bent. In the latter case, check which drop-out has to be bent in which direction, by checking carefully from behind and from the top when the wheel has been removed from the bike.

2. Clamp the drop-out to be straightened in the vise just below the location of the bend. Alternatively, you can use two 8-inch adjustable wrenches, one on either side of the bend.

3. Force the frame in the appropriate direction, using the bike (or the adjustable wrenches) for leverage.

Front derailleur lug detail.

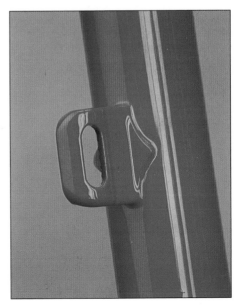

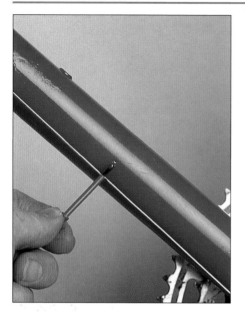

Touching up paint damage.

4. Check again and make any corrections that may be necessary.

Touching up Paint Damage

In off-road use, you can't help but scratch up your bike sometimes. At least once a season, it is worthwhile to touch up any nicks and scratches.

Tools and equipment:

touch-up paint; brush; cloth; sandpaper; paint thinner

Procedure:

1. Clean the bike thoroughly, to uncover any locations that may have to be touched up.

2. Sand down the area of the damage, folding the sandpaper into such a small pad that you remove as little good paint as possible.

3. Clean the area with a dry rag, then with paint thinner, treating only the small area immediately affected, and again with a clean, dry rag.

4. Dip the paint brush in the paint very sparingly, and treat only the area where the paint has been removed, minimizing any overlapping of paint that is still intact.

5. Clean the brush in paint thinner immediately after use and allow to dry suspended with the bristles down but not touching anything.

6. Allow to dry at least overnight before touching the frame again.

Notes:

1. If you can only get paint in a spraycan, spray a little in a bottle cap and dip the brush in it.

2. Do not touch any bonded or composite frame with paint thinner or other solvents, since that may weaken the joints.

CHAPTER 14

Accessories

Although most road bikes are ridden with no more than the essential equipment, some accessories can be added, significantly increasing the bike's utility value. Here is about all that can be said on the subject with regards to maintenance.

Bicycle Computer

Today, this is about the most common bicycle accessory, and these things are getting both cleverer and smaller every year. Select one that has the minimum number of knobs consistent with the functions you desire. Follow the manufacturer's instructions for installation, calibration, and maintenance.

Generally, the computer must be calibrated for the wheel size of your bike, measured accurately in mm between the road and the wheel axle of the loaded bike. Look for a model that is advertised as being waterproof and comes with a guarantee to back up this claim. If it is not, put a plastic bag over it in the rain and always take it off the bike when transporting the bike, e.g. on a car roofrack.

Bicycle computer installation.

To lubricate the lock, put oil on the key, rather than directly in the lock.

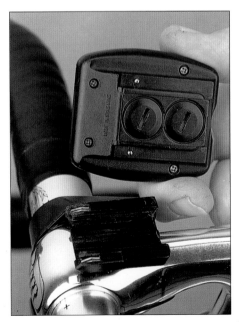

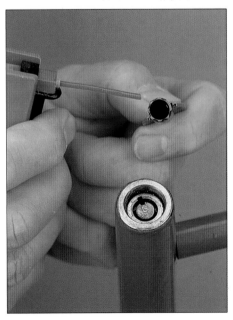

Lock

Whether you use a U-lock or a padlock with a separate chain or cable, you can keep it working with minimum maintenance. Put a drop of oil on the key and on the shackle that enters the lock, then open and close it.

Pump

At home, a big stand pump with hose connector and an integrated pressure gauge is most useful for fast and controlled tire inflation. On the bike, a smaller model will be needed. In addition to the standard versions intended for road bikes, there are special mountain bike pumps available. These have a larger diameter than the models intended for road bikes, allowing you to pump more air with each stroke of the pump, though at a slightly lower pressure.

Recently, CO_2 gas inflators have become popular, but they are more hassle than they are worth. Whatever type you use, get a pump with a head or hose connector to match the valves on your bike's tires. If you have to maintain bikes with different types of valves, buy an adaptor nipple to convert from one to the other.

Pump Maintenance

If the pump doesn't work properly, the leak is usually located at the head of the pump (the part that is put on the valve) or at the plunger inside the pump. On some pumps, the head can be replaced.

Tools and equipment:

screwdriver; lubricant

Procedure:

1. Tighten the screwed bushing that holds down the rubber sealing washer, or grommet, in the head of the pump.

2. If this doesn't solve the problem, unscrew it and check the grommet, replacing it if necessary (inflexible, cut, frayed, or enlarged hole); then screw the bushing back on.

3. If still no luck, unscrew the other end of the pump and check the condition of the leather or plastic plunger washer. If it is no longer flexible, impregnate it with any kind of vegetable or animal fat and make sure it is screwed down tight. If necessary, replace the plunger washer.

The pump head dismantled to expose the rubber grommet.

Lighting Equipment

For night-time riding on city streets, almost any light will do. However, under off-road conditions, no single light seems to be bright enough.

Although brighter lights can be obtained with separate rechargeable battery units, these are mainly used with mountain bikes (although they are just the ticket for fast riding on the road at night as well). The simplest acceptable lights for road bike use are powered by at least two D-cells each.

Battery Light Installation

This has to be very general advice, since there are so many makes and models, all differing in detail.

Tools and equipment:

6 mm crescent wrench; 3–5 mm Allen wrench; small screwdriver

Procedure:

Get the appropriate mounting hardware and install the light in such a way that it does not protrude beyond the bike more than necessary. The highest mounting position is generally the best, since it throws fewer confusing shadows and is more readily visible to others.

Although flashing LED-type rear lights are quite effective, a really big reflector mounted rather low is as visible as the best rear light to all other road users who have lighting themselves and who could endanger you from behind.

Battery Light Maintenance
This too has to be very general advice, but universally valid for all battery systems.

Tools and equipment:

spare batteries; spare bulb; sandpaper; battery terminal grease

Procedure:

1. Usually, when a battery light lets you down, it's a matter of a dead or dying battery. Always check that first, by trying the light with other batteries installed.

2. If that does not solve the problem, check whether the bulb is screwed in and contacts the terminal firmly. Scrape the contacts of bulb, battery, and switch to remove dirt or corrosion.

3. If still no luck, check the bulb and replace it if the filament is broken.

Simple battery-powered headlight opened up to expose batteries.

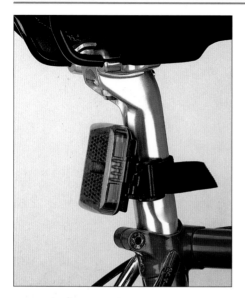

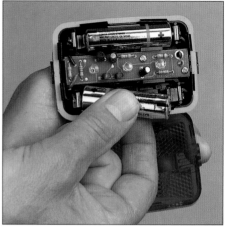

Flashing LED-type rear light.
Left:: installed.
Right: opened up to expose batteries.

4. To prevent corrosion of the contacts, lightly coat the terminals of all parts that carry electricity with battery terminal grease.

Reflectors

There are a few points to consider in the selection and maintenance of reflectors. In the first place, larger reflectors are more visible than smaller ones, all else being equal. Secondly, lighter colored reflectors are more visible than darker ones. Amber reflects twice as much light as red.

As for maintenance, wash the reflectors regularly with plenty of water. If water should leak inside the reflector, it condenses on the inside, making the reflector virtually blind. Replace a cracked reflector immediately. To check a reflector's operation, aim a light at it from a distance of 10 m (33 ft.), observing from a point close to the light source whether the reflector appears to light up brightly.

General Accessory Installation and Maintenance

The following simple rules will help you keep any other accessories on the bike in working order—or at least will prevent their interference with the safe operation of the bike.

1. Attachment must be at a minimum of two points, preferably off-set relative to one another.

2. If the accessory comes loose, don't just retighten it, but find a better attachment method.

3. If it gets damaged, remove, repair, or replace it immediately.

4. If it is a moving part, check whether it moves freely without resistance.

5. If it is a stationary part, keep it tightened and protected against rust.

Rob van der Plas is a resident of San Francisco and has lived in his native Holland, as well as in England and Germany, for many years before that. He is a professional engineer and a lifelong cycling enthusiast turned writer, and has written extensively on the subject for publishers on both sides of the Atlantic. He has written technical columns for *Bicycle Magazine* in Great Britain and *Fiets* in Holland.

In 1983 Penguin Books published his *Penguin Bicycle Handbook*, and his subsequent books were published by Bicycle Books, while several of his book are also available in translations into German, Dutch, Spanish, Swedish, Danish, and Polish.

Although he is interested in all aspects of the sport, he excels especially in preparing clear technical instructions, and several of his books attest to that: *Bicycle Technology*, *The Bicycle Repair Book*, *Roadside Bicycle Repair*, and *Mountain Bike Maintenance*.

He considers that, although there will always be a need for a general repair manual, today, the differences between the mountain bike and the road bike are so clearly drawn that it makes sense to treat them in separate books. The present book then, is the counterpiece to his popular *Mountain Bike Maintenance*, and provides the same kind of detailed and specific treatment for the road bike.

BIBLIOGRAPHY

Barnett, John. *Barnett's Manual*. 2nd ed. Brattleboro, VT: Vitesse Press, 1996.

Berto, Frank. *Upgrading Your Bike*. Emmaus, PA: Rodale Press, 1989.

Coles, C. W., H. T. Glenn, J. Allen. *Glenn's New Complete Bicycle Manual*. New York: Crown Publishers, 1989.

Editors of Bicycling Magazine. *Bicycling Magazine's Complete Guide to Bicycle Maintenance and Repair*. 2nd ed. Emmaus, PA: Rodale Press, 1994.

Snowling, Ken. *Cycle Mechanics*. Huddersfield (UK): Springfield Books, 1988.

Sutherland, Howard. *Sutherland's Handbook for Bicycle Mechanics*. 6th ed. Berkeley, CA: Sutherland Publications, 1996.

Van der Plas, Rob. *The Bicycle Repair Book*. 2nd. ed. San Francisco: Bicycle Books, 1993.

——— *Bicycle Technology*. San Francisco: Bicycle Books, 1992.

——— *Bicycle Repair Step by Step*. San Francisco: Bicycle Books, 1994; Huddersfield, U.K.: Springfield Books, 1993.

——— *Roadside Bicycle Repair*. San Francisco: Bicycle Books, 1995.

Index

NOTE: Bold page numbers
indicate illustrations

Other Titles Available from Bicycle Books

Title	Author	US Price
All Terrain Biking	Jim Zarka	$7.95
The Backroads of Holland	Helen Colijn	$12.95
The Bicycle Commuting Book	Rob van der Plas	$7.95
The Bicycle Fitness Book	Rob van der Plas	$7.95
The Bicycle Repair Book	Rob van der Plas	$9.95
Bicycle Repair Step by Step (color)*	Rob van der Plas	$14.95
Bicycle Technology	Rob van der Plas	$16.95
Bicycle Touring International	Kameel Nasr	$18.95
The Bicycle Touring Manual	Rob van der Plas	$16.95
Bicycling Fuel	Richard Rafoth	$9.95
Cycling Australia	Ian Duckworth	$14.95
Cycling Canada	John Smith	$12.95
Cycling in Cyberspace	Kienholz & Pavlak	$14.95
Cycling Europe	Nadine Slavinski	$12.95
Cycling Great Britain	Hughes & Cleary	$12.95
Cycling Kenya	Kathleen Bennett	$12.95
Cycling the Mediterranean	Kameel Nasr	$14.95
Cycling the San Francisco Bay Area	Carol O'Hare	$12.95
Cycling the U.S. Parks	Jim Clark	$12.95
A Guide to Cycling Injuries*	Domhnall MacAulley	$12.95
In High Gear (hardcover)	Samuel Abt	$21.95
The High Performance Heart	Maffetone & Mantell	$10.95
Mountain Bike Maintenance (color)	Rob van der Plas	$10.95
Mountain Bikes: Maint. & Repair*	Stevenson & Richards	$22.50
Mountain Biking the National Parks	Jim Clark	$12.95
Road Bike Maintenance	Rob van der Plas	$12.95
Roadside Bicycle Repair (color)	Rob van der Plas	$7.95
Tour of the Forest Bike Race (color)	H. E. Thomson	$9.95
Cycle History – 4th Intern. Conference Proceedings (hardcover)		$30.00
Cycle History – 5th Intern. Conference Proceedings (hardcover)		$45.00

Buy our books at your local book store or bike shop.

If you have difficulty obtaining our books elsewhere, we will be pleased to supply them by mail, but we must add $2.50 postage and handling, or $3.50 for priority mail (and California Sales Tax if mailed to a California address). Prepayment by check or credit card must be included.

Bicycle Books, Inc.
1282 - 7th Avenue
San Francisco, CA 94122, U.S.A.
Tel.   (415) 665-8214 or 1-800-468-8233
FAX (415) 753-8572

In Britain: Bicycle Books
463 Ashley Road
Poole, Dorset BH14 0AX
Tel.   (01202) 71 53 49
FAX   (01202) 73 61 91

---

* Books marked thus not available from Bicycle Books in the U.K.